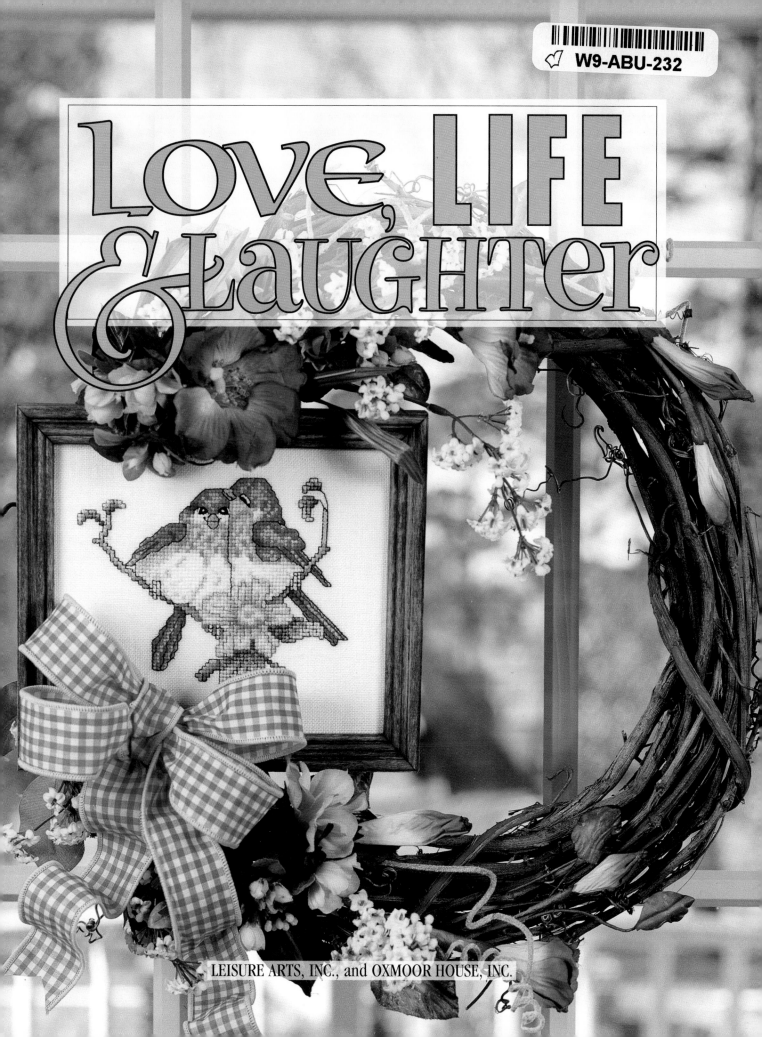

Love, LIFE & Laughter

LEISURE ARTS, INC., and OXMOOR HOUSE, INC.

2

LOVE, LIFE & LAUGHTER

*T*he secrets of a rich life — abundant love
and healthy doses of laughter — are celebrated
in this treasury of Leisure Arts' best cross-stitch
inspirations. Love, Life, and Laughter *is filled
with designs that are guaranteed to warm
hearts, uplift spirits, and induce lots of chuckles
along the way! Whether you're creating a day-
brightener for yourself or sharing a sentiment
with a loved one, you'll find clever ways
to express wit and wisdom through home
accents, clothing, and gifts. Our versatile
collection includes framed pieces and pillows,
as well as embellished shirts, aprons, and
towels. And there are plenty of easy ornaments,
mugs, and bookmarks that are great for quick-
to-stitch presents. For special occasions
or "just because," there's something for
everyone, from newlyweds to newborns —
and every friend in between. So turn the
page and discover just the right memento
to encourage, to advise, to amuse.*

Chart on page 142

EDITORIAL STAFF

Vice President and Editor-in-Chief:
Anne Van Wagner Childs
Executive Director: Sandra Graham Case
Editorial Director: Susan Frantz Wiles
Publications Director: Carla Bentley
Creative Art Director: Gloria Bearden
Senior Graphics Art Director: Melinda Stout

EDITORIAL
Managing Editor: Linda L. Trimble
Senior Associate Editor: Terri Leming Davidson
Associate Editors: Stacey Robertson Marshall
and Janice Teipen Wojcik

TECHNICAL
Project Editor: Connie White Irby
Production Assistant: Martha H. Carle

ART
Book/Magazine Graphics Art Director: Diane M. Hugo
Senior Graphics Illustrator: Guniz Jernigan
Production Graphics Illustrators: Fred Bassett,
Linda Culp Calhoun, Bridgett Shrum, and Rhonda K. Stout

BUSINESS STAFF

Publisher: Bruce Akin
Vice President, Marketing: Guy A. Crossley
Vice President and General Manager: Thomas L. Carlisle
Retail Sales Director: Richard Tignor
Vice President, Retail Marketing: Pam Stebbins
Retail Marketing Director: Margaret Sweetin
Retail Customer Service Manager: Carolyn Pruss
General Merchandise Manager: Cathy Laird
Vice President, Finance: Tom Siebenmorgen
Distribution Director: Rob Thieme

Library of Congress Catalog Number 98-65090
Hardcover ISBN 1-57486-112-3
Softcover ISBN 1-57486-113-1

Table of Contents

Love
MUCH

A gentle embrace, a lingering glance, the soft melody of whispered sweet nothings — the warmth of love adds richness to our lives and lilt to our laughter. This touching collection celebrates love in all its splendid dimensions, from enduring friendships to tender romance to precious and poignant sentiments twixt parent and child. With a tapestry-like floral border, the pretty passage in Reflections on Marriage *creates a thought-provoking remembrance that promises to become an heirloom.*

ove does not consist
n gazing at each other,
t in looking together
the same direction.
Saint Exupéry

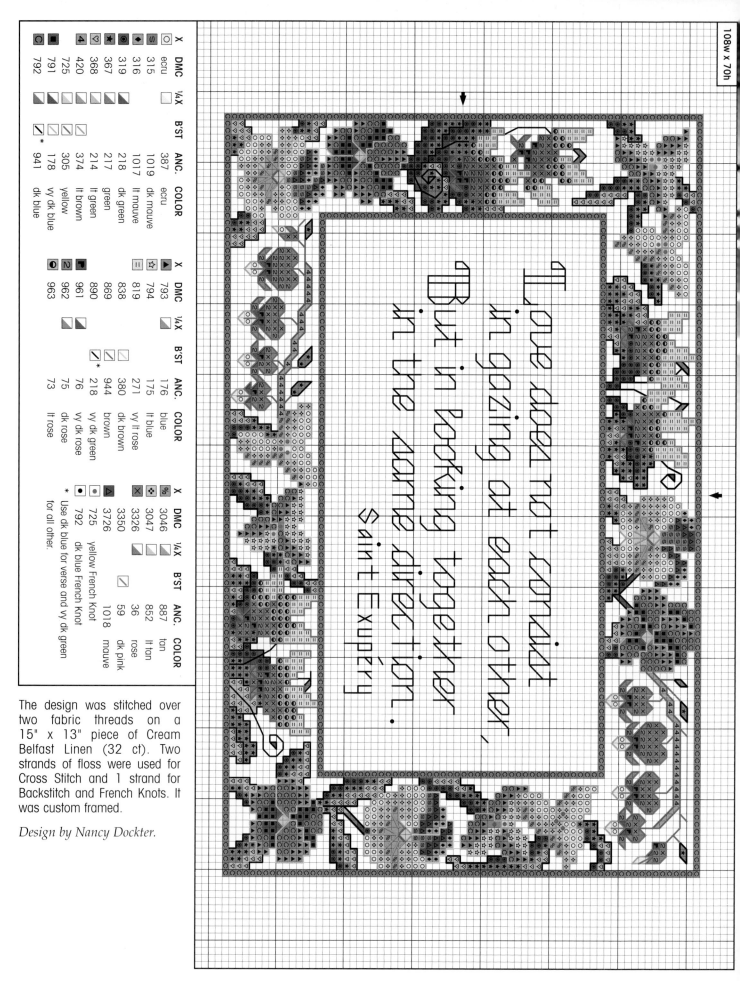

X	DMC	ANC.	COLOR
	ecru	387	ecru
	315	1019	dk mauve
	316	1017	lt mauve
	319	218	dk green
	367	217	green
	368	214	lt green
	420	374	lt brown
	725	305	yellow
	791	178	vy dk blue
	792	941	dk blue

1/4X · B'ST

X	DMC	ANC.	COLOR
	793	176	blue
	794	175	lt blue
	819	271	vy lt rose
	838	380	dk brown
	869	944	brown
	890	218	vy dk green
	961	76	vy dk rose
	962	75	dk rose
	963	73	lt rose

1/4X · B'ST

X	DMC	ANC.	COLOR
	3046	887	tan
	3047	852	lt tan
	3326	36	rose
	3350	59	dk pink
	3726	1018	mauve
	725		yellow French Knot
	792		dk blue French Knot

* Use dk blue for verse and vy dk green for all other.

The design was stitched over two fabric threads on a 15" x 13" piece of Cream Belfast Linen (32 ct). Two strands of floss were used for Cross Stitch and 1 strand for Backstitch and French Knots. It was custom framed.

Design by Nancy Dockter.

Abloom with flowers and romance, this delicate ornament is a lovely token for a bride-to-be. She's sure to pick a special spot in her home for this handmade gift from the heart!

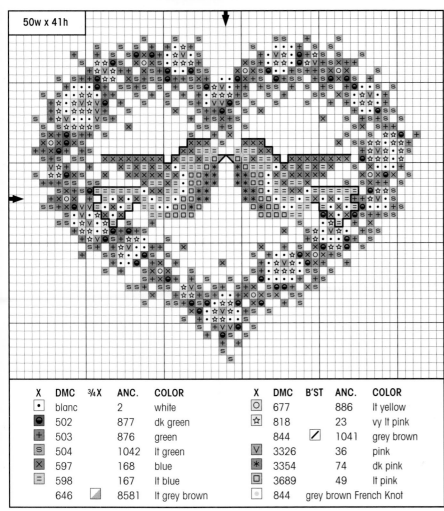

50w x 41h

The design was stitched on an 8" x 7" piece of Mint Green Damask Aida (14 ct). Two strands of floss were used for Cross Stitch and 1 strand for Backstitch and French Knots. It was made into a heart-shaped ornament.

For each heart pattern, fold tracing paper in half and place fold on dashed line of pattern; trace. Cut out traced pattern. Draw around small heart pattern twice on adhesive board and twice on batting; cut out. Remove paper from adhesive board piece and adhere one batting piece to each adhesive board piece. Center large heart pattern over stitched piece; draw around pattern. Cut out stitched piece. Cut backing fabric same size as stitched piece.

For ornament front, clip 3/8" into edges of stitched piece at 1/2" intervals. Center stitched piece over batting side of one adhesive board piece; fold edges to wrong side and glue in place. Repeat with backing fabric and remaining adhesive board piece for ornament back.

Referring to photo for placement, glue a 12" length of 1/4"w flat lace to wrong side of ornament front; glue a 12" length of 5/8"w flat lace to wrong side of 1/4"w lace. Glue a 12" length of pearl beads to right side of 1/4"w lace against edge of heart.

For hanger, fold a 9" length of 1/4"w satin ribbon in half and glue ends to wrong side of ornament front at top of heart. Glue wrong sides of ornament front and back together. Glue a small ceramic rose and leaves to center top of heart.

Design by Diane Brakefield.

X	DMC	3/4X	ANC.	COLOR	X	DMC	B'ST	ANC.	COLOR
•	blanc		2	white	○	677		886	lt yellow
◕	502		877	dk green	☆	818		23	vy lt pink
+	503		876	green		844	◢	1041	grey brown
S	504		1042	lt green	V	3326		36	pink
X	597		168	blue	*	3354		74	dk pink
=	598		167	lt blue	□	3689		49	lt pink
	646	◢	8581	lt grey brown	◉	844			grey brown French Knot

Heartfelt motifs and simple words add to the charm of this old-fashioned sampler. The piece offers a quiet reflection on the things we should hold dear.

To love and
be loved is
the greatest
joy on earth.

Design by
Linda Culp Calhoun.

X	DMC	B'ST	ANC.	COLOR	X	DMC	ANC.	COLOR
◐	319		218	vy dk green	▣	3350	59	vy dk rose
✚	320	╱	215	green	★	3354	74	lt rose
◈	367		217	dk green	✕	3731	76	dk rose
⊟	368		214	lt green	⋁	3733	75	rose
✳	642	╱	392	beige	◆	3743	869	lt purple
C	822		390	cream	⦿	Mill Hill Antique Seed		
☆	3041		871	dk purple		Beads #03021		
▲	3042		870	purple	⦿	Mill Hill Frosted Seed		
⊝	3047		852	yellow		Beads #62024		

The **entire design** was stitched over two fabric threads on a 12" x 15" piece of Cream Belfast Linen (32 ct). Two strands of floss were used for Cross Stitch and 1 strand for Backstitch. It was custom framed.

To attach beads, refer to chart for bead placement and sew each bead in place using 1 strand of embroidery floss and a needle that will pass through the bead.

One **floral motif** (refer to photo) was stitched over two fabric threads on a 6" square of Cream Belfast Linen (32 ct). Two strands of floss were used for Cross Stitch. It was inserted in the lid of a porcelain jar (2³/₄" dia. opening).

The romantic at heart will cherish our dainty throw pillow with its message of love stitched on a cheery yellow background. We finished it with frilly ruffles for a pretty decorative look.

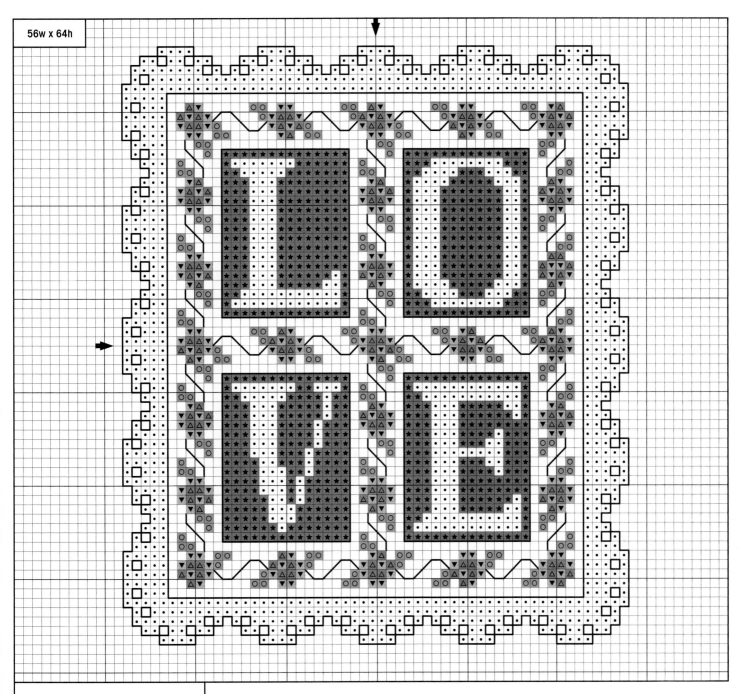

56w x 64h

X	DMC	B'ST	ANC.	COLOR
•	blanc		2	white
	318	∕	399	grey
△	335		38	dk pink
▼	776		24	pink
★	813		161	blue
	912	∕*	209	green
○	954		203	lt green
* Use 2 strands of floss.				

The design was stitched on a 13" x 14" piece of Yellow Aida (14 ct). Three strands of floss were used for Cross Stitch and 1 strand for Backstitch unless otherwise noted in color key. It was made into a pillow.

Note: Use a 1/2" seam allowance for all seams.

For pillow front, trim stitched piece 1 1/2" larger than design on all sides. Cut a piece of backing fabric the same size as stitched piece.

For cording, press one end of a 2" x 30" bias fabric strip 1/2" to wrong side. Center a 30" length of 1/4" dia. cord on wrong side of bias strip. Matching long edges, fold strip over cord. Using zipper foot, baste along length of strip close to cord; trim seam allowance to 1/2". Matching raw edges and beginning at center bottom, pin cording to right side of pillow front. Clip 3/8" into seam allowances at corners. Trim ends of cord to meet. With folded edge on top, overlap fabric over ends of cord. Baste cording in place.

For fabric and lace ruffle, match right sides and short edges of a 5" x 56" piece of fabric. Sew short edges together; press seam open.

With wrong sides together, match raw edges and press ruffle in half. Sew short edges of a 56" length of 1"w flat lace together; press seam open. Matching raw edges of ruffle and straight edge of lace, baste 3/8" and 1/4" from raw edge. Pull basting threads, gathering ruffle to fit edge of pillow front. Matching raw edges, pin ruffle to right side of pillow front over cording; baste in place.

Matching right sides and leaving an opening for turning, sew stitched piece and backing fabric together. Trim corners diagonally; turn pillow right side out. Stuff pillow with fiberfill; sew final closure by hand.

Design by Jane Chandler.

13

The beautiful blooms that welcome spring are testament to God's divine love! Embellished with flower-entwined letters, this vibrant sweatshirt proclaims that Fatherly affection.

X	DMC	B'ST	ANC.	COLOR		X	DMC	¼X	B'ST	ANC.	COLOR
✦	208		110	purple			666		╱	46	dk coral
✳	209		109	lt purple		⊖	700			228	green
	550	╱	102	dk purple		◆	703			238	lt green
	601	╱	57	dk pink		☐	743			302	yellow
★	603		62	pink		◉	970			316	orange
	608	╱	332	dk orange		▲	3801	◪		35	coral

The design was stitched over a 14" x 13" piece of 8.5 mesh waste canvas on a sweatshirt. Six strands of floss were used for Cross Stitch and 2 strands for Backstitch. See Working on Waste Canvas, page 144.

Design by Terrece Beesley.

Pretty posies and tender "toe-sies" are a wonderful way to personalize a cross-stitched birth certificate. Tiny footprints are easily added along with baby's name and measurements.

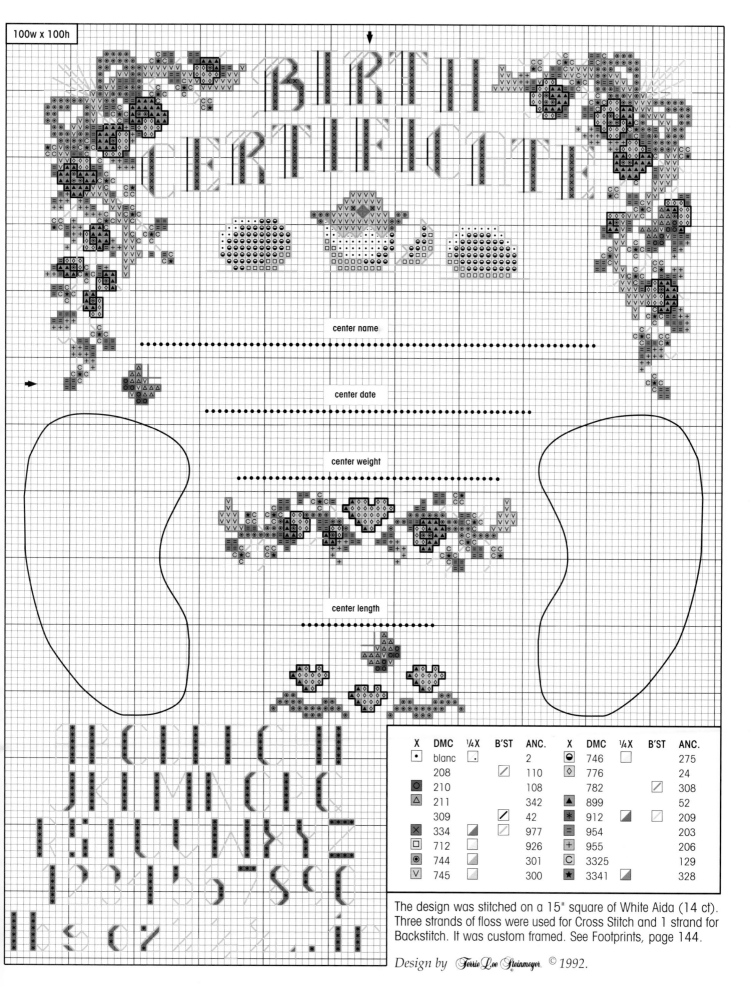

100w x 100h

center name

center date

center weight

center length

X	DMC	¼X	B'ST	ANC.	X	DMC	¼X	B'ST	ANC.
•	blanc	•		2	☉	746			275
	208		/	110	◇	776			24
○	210			108		782		/	308
△	211			342	▲	899			52
	309		/	42	✳	912	◩		209
✕	334	◩	/	977	=	954			203
▢	712			926	+	955			206
◉	744			301	C	3325			129
∨	745			300	★	3341	◩		328

The design was stitched on a 15" square of White Aida (14 ct). Three strands of floss were used for Cross Stitch and 1 strand for Backstitch. It was custom framed. See Footprints, page 144.

Design by Terrie Lee Steinmeyer. © 1992.

Express your wishes for a long and loving marriage with a handmade wedding gift — our pretty pillow! Sharing the simple truths found in I Corinthians, the design will convey your heartfelt sentiments to a special couple.

Love is patient... love is kind. It does not envy, it does not boast, it is not proud. It is not rude, it is not selfish, it is not easily angered, it keeps no record of wrongs. Love does not delight in evil, but with the truth rejoices. It always protects, always trusts, always hopes, always perseveres. And now these three remain: faith, hope, and love. But the greatest of these three is LOVE. I CORINTHIANS 13:4-7 & 13.

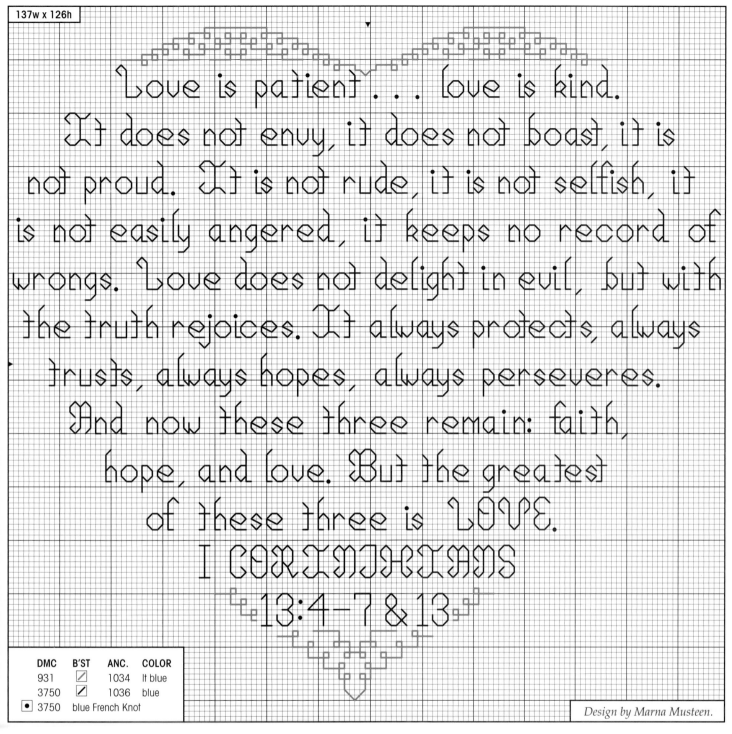

137w x 126h

Love is patient . . . love is kind. It does not envy, it does not boast, it is not proud. It is not rude, it is not selfish, it is not easily angered, it keeps no record of wrongs. Love does not delight in evil, but with the truth rejoices. It always protects, always trusts, always hopes, always perseveres. And now these three remain: faith, hope, and love. But the greatest of these three is LOVE. I CORINTHIANS 13:4-7 & 13

DMC	B'ST	ANC.	COLOR
931	✎	1034	lt blue
3750	✎	1036	blue
● 3750			blue French Knot

Design by Marna Musteen.

The design was stitched over two fabric threads on a 15" x 14" piece of Antique White Lugana (25 ct). One strand of floss was used for Backstitch and French Knots. It was made into a pillow.

Note: Use a 1/2" seam allowance for all seams.

For pillow front, trim stitched piece to 13 1/2" x 12 1/2". Cut a piece of backing fabric the same size as stitched piece.

For cording, press one end of a 2" x 54" bias fabric strip 1/2" to wrong side. Center a 54" length of 1/4" dia. cord on wrong side of bias strip. Matching long edges, fold strip over cord. Using zipper foot, baste along length of strip close to cord; trim seam allowance to 1/2". Matching raw edges and beginning at center bottom, pin cording to right side of pillow front. Clip 3/8" into seam

allowances at corners. Trim ends of cord to meet. With folded edge on top, overlap fabric over ends of cord. Baste cording in place.

For ruffle, match right sides and short edges of an 8" x 105" piece of fabric. Sew short edges together; press seam open. With wrong sides together, match raw edges and press ruffle in half. To gather ruffle, baste 3/8" and 1/4" from raw edge. Pull basting threads, gathering ruffle to fit edge of pillow front. Matching raw edges, pin ruffle to right side of pillow front over cording; baste in place.

Matching right sides and leaving an opening for turning, sew stitched piece and backing fabric together. Trim corners diagonally, turn pillow right side out. Stuff pillow with fiberfill; sew final closure by hand.

The unspoken bond between true friends provides the strength we need to weather any storm. Presented to such a treasured friend, this touching scene honors that unique love.

64w x 91h

X	DMC	1/4X	B'ST	ANC.	COLOR
◉	208			110	dk lavender
▢	210	◩		108	lavender
▽	402	◩	◲	1047	copper
■	413	◪	◲	401	grey
◖	666	◪		46	red
+	745	◲		300	yellow
❖	754	◲		1012	flesh
◆	792	◪	◲	941	dk blue
✳	798	◩		131	blue
▥	799			136	lt blue

X	DMC	1/4X	B'ST	ANC.	COLOR
◈	800	◲		144	vy lt blue
	839		◲	360	beige brown
◆	840	◪		379	lt beige brown
◯	841	◲		378	vy lt beige brown
▲	910	◪	◲	229	green
★	912	◩		209	lt green
♡	948	◲		1011	lt flesh
=	3716	◲		25	pink
◦	792				dk blue French Knot
●	839				beige brown French Knot

The design was stitched on an 11" x 14" piece of White Aida (14 ct). Three strands of floss were used for Cross Stitch, and 1 strand for Backstitch and French Knots. It was inserted in a purchased frame (5" x 7") opening).

Design by Holly DeFount.

A quartet of kindness, these easy designs are quick to make for any gift-giving occasion. Tuck one in a pretty frame and share it with a friend!

1. 32w x 28h

A FRIEND IS THE HOPE OF THE

2. 39w x 38h

The best thing to give a friend is your

3. 39w x 35h

FRIENDSHIP MAKES THE rough road smooth

4. 36w x 36h

If friends were flowers, I'd pick you.

X	DMC	¼X	B'ST	ANC.	COLOR	X	DMC	¼X	B'ST	ANC.	COLOR
•	blanc			2	white		798		╱	131	dk blue
◉	223			895	mauve	◆	809	◢		130	blue
✕	224			893	lt mauve	△	899			52	pink
	309		╱	42	vy dk pink		930		╱	1035	dk grey blue
▼	433		╱	358	dk brown	%	931			1034	grey blue
◆	434	◢		310	brown	4	932	◢		1033	lt grey blue
✳	436	◢		1045	lt brown	⊠	3325			129	lt blue
	562		╱	210	green	☆	3326			36	lt pink
▽	563	◢		208	lt green		3722		╱	1027	dk mauve
◉	743	◢		302	yellow		3731		╱	76	dk pink
▢	745	◢		300	lt yellow	✧	3753	◢		1031	vy lt blue
=	754	◢		1012	flesh	⦿	798				dk blue French Knot
	783		╱	307	gold	●	930				dk grey blue French Knot

Designs #1 and **#2** were each stitched on a 9" square of White Aida (14 ct). **Designs #3** and **#4** were each stitched on a 9" square of Antique White Aida (14 ct). Three strands of floss were used for Cross Stitch and 1 strand for Backstitch and French Knots. They were custom framed.

Designs by Holly DeFount.

KOOLER DESIGN STUDIO

23

A bit of garden wisdom teaches us that from our seeds of kindness, come the fruit of love. Hang the rustic piece near the door for sage advice to remember on the go.

those who
plant
kindness
gather
Love~

24

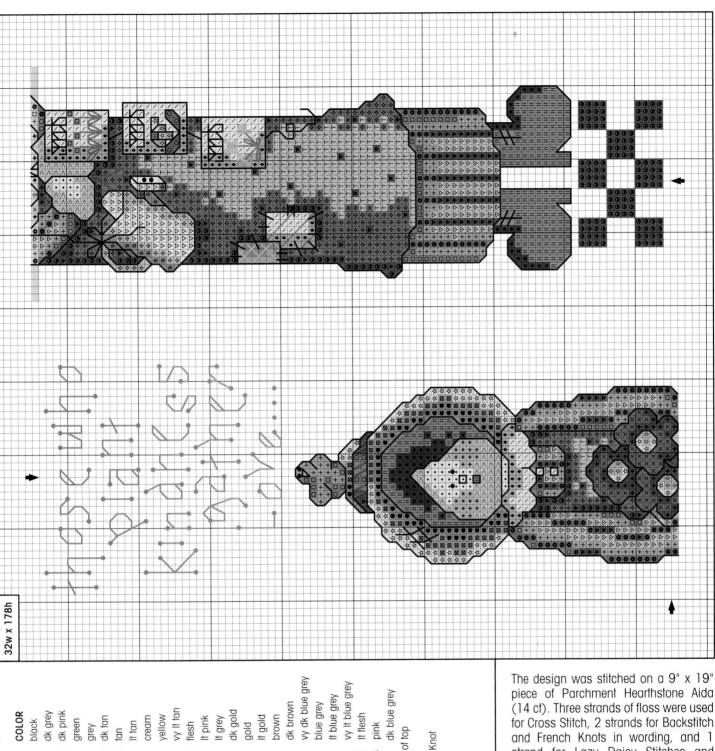

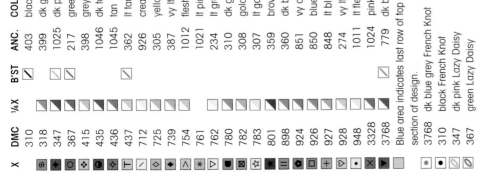

32w x 178h

X	DMC	¹⁄₄X	B'ST	ANC.	COLOR
⊞	310	◼	◥	403	black
✦	318	◼		399	dk grey
❖	347	◼	◥	1025	dk pink
⊙	367	◼	◥	217	green
◗	415	◼		398	grey
◐	435	◼		1046	dk tan
◖	436	◼		1045	tan
T	437	◻		362	lt tan
╱	712	◻		926	cream
◇	725	◻		305	yellow
◆	739	◼	◥	387	vy lt tan
∧	754	◻		1012	flesh
✳	761	◼		1021	lt pink
▷	762	◼		234	lt grey
◨	780	◼		310	dk gold
⊠	782	◻		308	gold
☆	783	◼		307	lt gold
★	801	◼		359	brown
▬	898	◼		360	dk brown
⊟	924	◼		851	vy dk blue grey
◓	926	◻		850	blue grey
□	927	◻		848	lt blue grey
+	928	◻		274	vy lt blue grey
▷	948	◻		1011	lt flesh
•	3328	◼		1024	pink
✕	3768	◼	◥	779	dk blue grey
▶					
▨					

Blue area indicates last row of top
section of design.

◉	3768	dk blue grey French Knot
●	310	black French Knot
◌	347	dk pink Lazy Daisy
◌	367	green Lazy Daisy

The design was stitched on a 9" x 19" piece of Parchment Hearthstone Aida (14 ct). Three strands of floss were used for Cross Stitch, 2 strands for Backstitch and French Knots in wording, and 1 strand for Lazy Daisy Stitches and remaining Backstitch and French Knots. It was inserted in a paddle frame (3" x 13" opening).

Design by Pat Olson.

Edged with a simple nosegay and sprays of forget-me-nots, this touching verse conveys a tender sentiment. It reminds us that even when cherished ones can't be near, their love is never far away.

Forget me not
while we're apart
And keep me always
in your heart

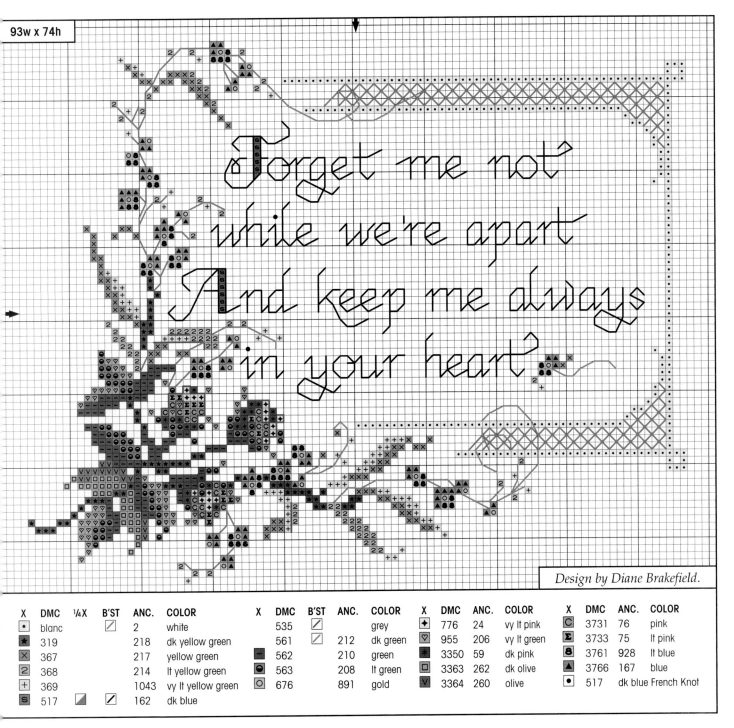

Forget me not
while we're apart
And keep me always
in your heart

Design by Diane Brakefield.

X	DMC	¼X	B'ST	ANC.	COLOR
•	blanc		◿	2	white
★	319			218	dk yellow green
✕	367			217	yellow green
2	368			214	lt yellow green
+	369			1043	vy lt yellow green
S	517	◢	◿	162	dk blue

X	DMC	B'ST	ANC.	COLOR
	535	◿		grey
	561	◿	212	dk green
⊟	562		210	green
◉	563		208	lt green
○	676		891	gold

X	DMC	ANC.	COLOR
✦	776	24	vy lt pink
♡	955	206	vy lt green
✳	3350	59	dk pink
▢	3363	262	dk olive
V	3364	260	olive

X	DMC	ANC.	COLOR
C	3731	76	pink
Σ	3733	75	lt pink
8	3761	928	lt blue
▲	3766	167	blue
•	517		dk blue French Knot

The **entire design** was stitched over two fabric threads on a 14" x 13" piece of Antique White Belfast Linen (32 ct). Two strands of floss were used for Cross Stitch and 1 strand for Backstitch and French Knots. Blanc Backstitch was worked in long stitches. It was custom framed.

The **floral design only** (refer to photo) was stitched over two fabric threads on a 9" square of Antique White Belfast Linen (32 ct) with design placed 1¼" from left side and 1¼" from bottom edge of fabric piece. Two strands of floss were used for Cross Stitch and 1 strand for Backstitch. It was made into a pillow.

Note: Use a ½" seam allowance for all seams.

For pillow back, cut a 9" square of fabric.

For cording, press one end of a 2½" x 38" bias fabric strip ½" to wrong side. Center a 38" length of ¼" dia. cord on wrong side of bias strip. Matching long edges, fold strip over cord. Using zipper foot, baste along length of strip close to cord; trim seam

allowance to ½". Matching raw edges and beginning at center bottom, pin cording to right side of pillow front. Clip ³⁄₈" into seam allowances at corners. Trim ends of cord to meet. With folded edge on top, overlap fabric over ends of cord. Baste cording in place.

For ruffle, match right sides and short edges of an 5" x 80" piece of fabric. Sew short edges together; press seam open. With wrong sides together, match raw edges and press ruffle in half. To gather ruffle, baste ³⁄₈" and ¼" from raw edge. Pull basting threads, gathering ruffle to fit edge of pillow front. Matching raw edges, pin ruffle to right side of pillow front over cording; baste in place.

Matching right sides and leaving an opening for turning, sew stitched piece and backing fabric together. Trim corners diagonally; turn pillow right side out. Stuff pillow with fiberfill; sew final closure by hand.

Love is for the birds — a sweet pair of bluebirds, that is! This affectionate couple, perched innocently on a flowered branch, shares a tender moment.

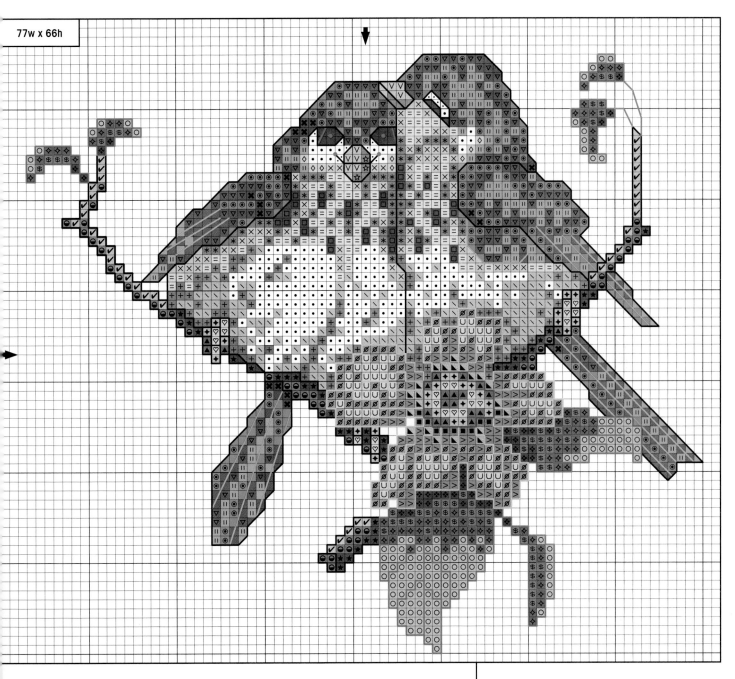

X	DMC	¼X	B'ST	ANC.	COLOR		X	DMC	¼X	B'ST	ANC.	COLOR
•	blanc	◩	◪	2	white		✦	676			891	gold
▣	310	◪	◪	403	black		♡	677			886	lt gold
	311		◪	148	dk blue			680		◪	901	vy dk gold
✖	312	◪		979	blue		▲	729			890	dk gold
◉	322	◪		978	lt blue		✕	758	◪		882	lt rust
	326		◪	59	dk rose		◇	775			128	vy lt baby blue
▽	334	◪		977	dk baby blue		∅	776			24	pink
■	335			38	rose		U	818			23	vy lt pink
▣	356	◪		5975	dk rust		\	822	◪		390	vy lt beige grey
★	434	◪		310	dk brown		◣	899			52	lt rose
◒	435			1046	brown		☆	976	◪		1001	copper
✔	437	◪		362	vy lt brown		V	977			1002	lt copper
	500		◪	683	vy dk green		‖	3325	◪		129	lt baby blue
✦	501			878	dk green		>	3326			36	vy lt rose
$	502			877	green		✳	3778	◪		1013	rust
◈	503			876	lt green		=	3779	◪		868	vy lt rust
○	504			1042	vy lt green		⊙	blanc				white French Knot
+	644	◪		830	lt beige grey		●	310				black French Knot

The design was stitched over two fabric threads on a 12" x 11" piece of Antique White Cashel Linen® (28 ct). Three strands of floss were used for Cross Stitch and 1 strand for Backstitch and French Knots. It was inserted in a purchased frame (6" x 7" opening) and attached to a wreath.

Design by Carolyn Shores Wright.
Artwork designs are reproduced under license from © Arts Uniq'®, Inc., Cookeville, TN

29

A simple border of entwined hearts is a lovely frame for this charming sentiment, which evokes the unbreakable bond between trusted friends.

71w x 101h

X	DMC	B'ST	ANC.	COLOR
*	316	/	1017	rose
S	503		876	green
□	758		882	peach
X	932		1033	blue
C	3041		871	mauve
=	3078		292	yellow
●	316			rose French Knot

The **entire design** was stitched over two fabric threads on a 13" x 15" piece of Cream Belfast Linen (32 ct). Two strands of floss were used for Cross Stitch and 1 strand for Backstitch and French Knots. It was custom framed.

The **border only** (refer to photo) was repeated and stitched over two fabric threads on a 12" x 20" piece of Cream Belfast Linen (32 ct) with the bottom of design 1½" from one short edge. Two strands of floss were used for Cross Stitch. It was made into a towel.

For towel, fold each edge ¼" to wrong side; press. Fold ¼" again; hem. Cut a 12" length of 1¼"w pregathered lace. Press short edges of lace ¼" to wrong side; press short edges ¼" to wrong side again and hem. With right side of lace and wrong side of towel facing, sew gathered edge of lace to bottom edge of towel.

Design by Mary Scott.

31

These miniature mementos are nice little ways to honor your parents. Featuring reverent Bible verses and classic floral motifs, these framed pieces are ideal gifts for Mother's Day and Father's Day.

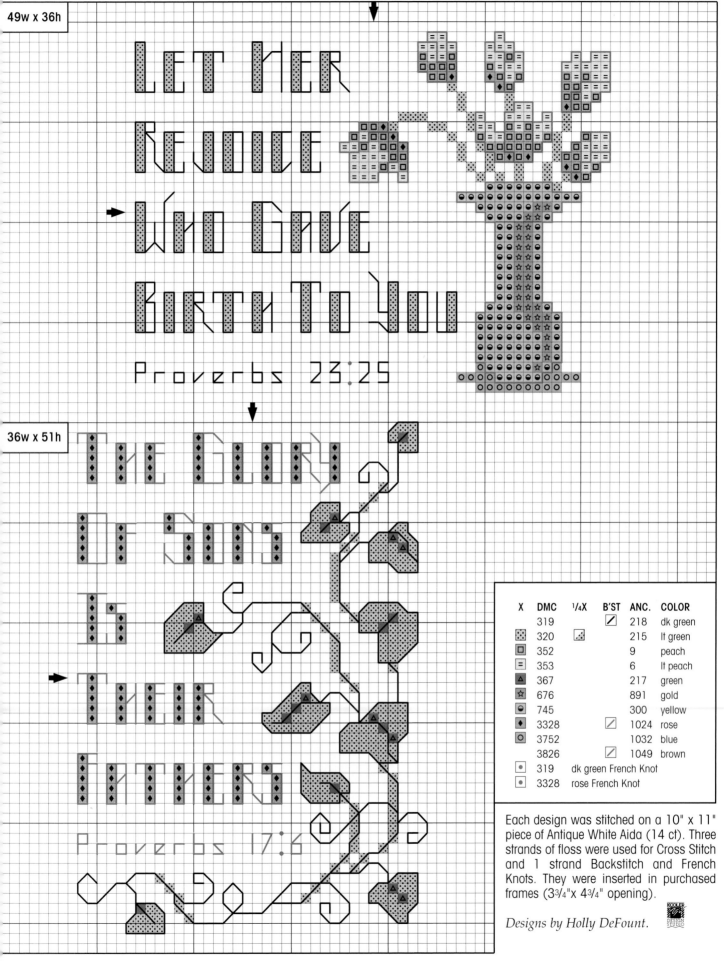

49w x 36h

LET HER
REJOICE
WHO GAVE
BIRTH TO YOU
Proverbs 23:25

36w x 51h

THE GLORY
OF SONS
IS
THEIR
FATHERS
Proverbs 17:6

X	DMC	¼X	B'ST	ANC.	COLOR
	319		╱	218	dk green
⊡	320	⊡		215	lt green
⊡	352			9	peach
=	353			6	lt peach
▲	367			217	green
☆	676			891	gold
◕	745			300	yellow
◆	3328		╱	1024	rose
◉	3752			1032	blue
	3826		╱	1049	brown
⊙	319		dk green French Knot		
⊙	3328		rose French Knot		

Each design was stitched on a 10" x 11" piece of Antique White Aida (14 ct). Three strands of floss were used for Cross Stitch and 1 strand Backstitch and French Knots. They were inserted in purchased frames (3³⁄₄"x 4³⁄₄" opening).

Designs by Holly DeFount.

This sweet little memento is a quick gift for newlyweds. Designed to fit in a purchased frame, it can be personalized with the names of the bride and groom and their wedding date.

X	DMC	¼X	B'ST	ANC.	COLOR
•	blanc			2	white
$	334		✓	977	dk blue
	335		✓	38	dk pink
*	413		✓	401	grey
	433		✓	358	dk brown
+	435			1046	brown
■	561		✓	212	dk green
Σ	562			210	green
%	744			301	yellow
8	945			881	peach
♥	3325			129	blue
Π	3326			36	pink

The design was stitched on a 9" square of Antique White Aida (14 ct). Three strands of floss were used for Cross Stitch and 1 strand for Backstitch. It was inserted in a purchased frame (4" square opening).

Design by Linda Gillum.

40w x 40h

center name   center name

center date

Bordered with forget-me-nots, this familiar verse speaks eloquently of the bonds of friendship. It's fashioned into a lacy cushion, which will be a cherished accent for a dressing table.

77w x 61h

X	DMC	B'ST	COLOR
5	334		dk blue
⊖	452		grey
C	453		lt grey
	500	╱	vy dk green
⊠	501		dk green
O	502		green
✳	504		lt green
☆	742		gold
=	775		lt blue
	930	╱	vy dk blue
△	3051		olive green
+	3325		blue
●	930		vy dk blue French Knot

The design was stitched over two fabric threads on a 9" x 8" piece of Antique White Belfast Linen (32 ct). Two strands of floss were used for Cross Stitch and 1 strand for Backstitch and French Knots. It was made into a pillow. See Pillow Finishing, page 144.

Design by Diane Brakefield.

This country scene captures the peaceful beauty of a crisp autumn day. The tender words remind us to trust our hearts to lead us safely on our way.

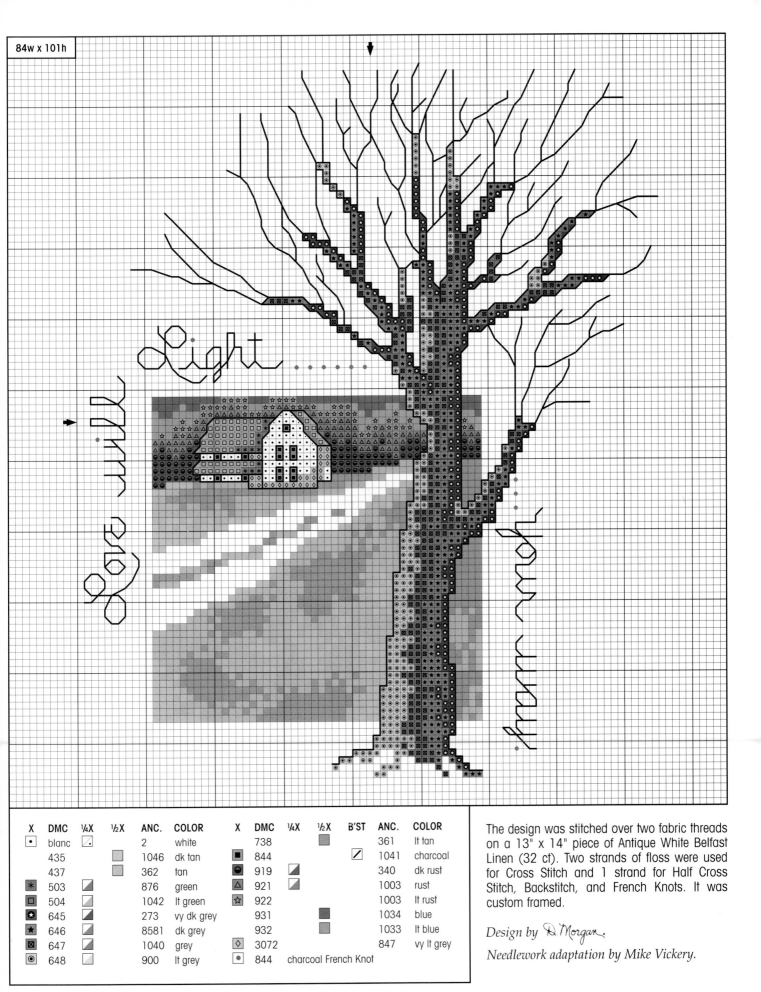

84w x 101h

X	DMC	¼X	½X	ANC.	COLOR	X	DMC	¼X	½X	B'ST	ANC.	COLOR
•	blanc			2	white		738				361	lt tan
	435			1046	dk tan	■	844			/	1041	charcoal
	437			362	tan	●	919				340	dk rust
✳	503			876	green	△	921				1003	rust
□	504			1042	lt green	☆	922				1003	lt rust
❂	645			273	vy dk grey		931				1034	blue
★	646			8581	dk grey		932				1033	lt blue
⊠	647			1040	grey	◇	3072				847	vy lt grey
◉	648			900	lt grey	●	844					charcoal French Knot

The design was stitched over two fabric threads on a 13" x 14" piece of Antique White Belfast Linen (32 ct). Two strands of floss were used for Cross Stitch and 1 strand for Half Cross Stitch, Backstitch, and French Knots. It was custom framed.

Design by D. Morgan.
Needlework adaptation by Mike Vickery.

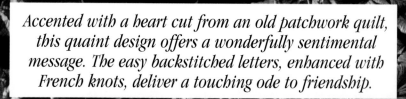

Accented with a heart cut from an old patchwork quilt, this quaint design offers a wonderfully sentimental message. The easy backstitched letters, enhanced with French knots, deliver a touching ode to friendship.

Love is the thread that joins friends together.

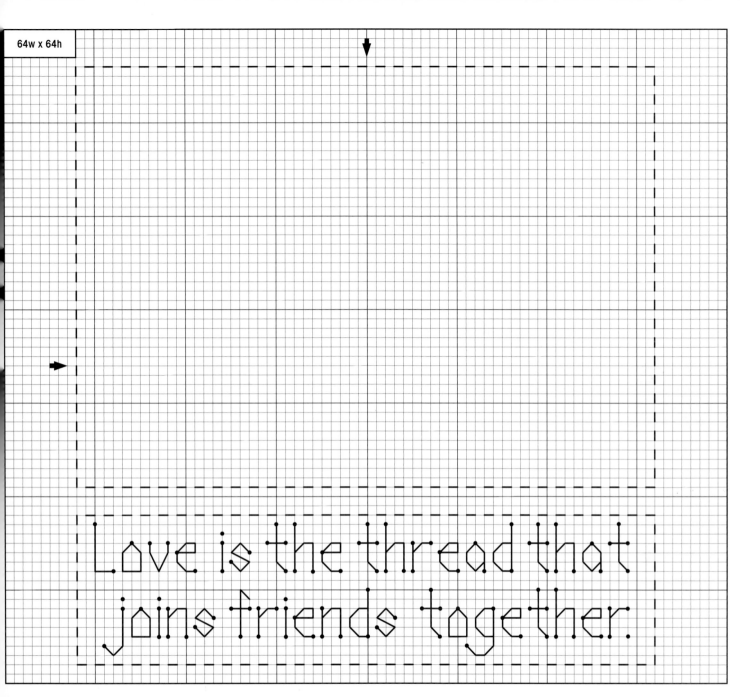

64w x 64h

Love is the thread that joins friends together.

The design was stitched on a 9" square of Beige Aida (14 ct). One strand of floss was used for Backstitch and French Knots (we used DMC 3750). It was inserted in a purchased frame (6" square opening).

For heart, trace pattern onto tracing paper and cut out. Following manufacturer's instructions, center and apply a 5½" square of paper-backed fusible web to the wrong side of a 6" square quilt scrap. Do **not** remove paper backing. Center pattern on paper-backing side of quilt scrap; draw around pattern and cut out. Remove paper backing. Following manufacturer's instructions, refer to photo for placement and fuse heart to stitched piece. Using 4 strands of floss (we used DMC 3750), work Blanket Stitch around heart.

Design by Sandy Gervais.

Blanket Stitch: Bring needle up at 1. Go down at 2 and come up at 3, keeping floss below point of needle (**Fig. 1**). Continue in this manner, keeping stitches even (**Fig. 2**).

Fig. 1

Fig. 2

Written for her beloved husband, the tender words of Elizabeth Barrett Browning will warm your dear one's heart. The simple lettering in the design is illuminated with a column of dainty flowers.

How do I love thee?
Let me count the ways.
I love thee to the depth
And breadth and height
My soul can reach...
I love thee with the breath,
Smiles, tears, of all my life!
And if God choose,
I shall but love thee
Better after death.

E. B. Browning

75w x 91h

How do I love thee?
Let me count the ways.
I love thee to the depth
And breadth and height
My soul can reach...
I love thee with the breath,
Smiles, tears, of all my life!
And if God choose,
I shall but love thee
Better after death.

E. B. Browning

X	DMC	¼X	B'ST	ANC.	COLOR
	347		◨	1025	red
	370	◨	◨	855	beige
♡	520	◨		862	dk green
S	676			891	yellow
+	677			886	lt yellow
▲	729			890	dk yellow
◉	760			1022	rose
×	761			1021	lt rose
	780		◨	310	vy dk yellow
◔	930	◨		1035	dk blue

X	DMC	¼X	B'ST	ANC.	COLOR
△	931			1034	blue
2	932	◨		1033	lt blue
	934		◨	862	vy dk green
✱	3021		◨	905	brown
✳	3328			1024	vy dk rose
★	3363	◨		262	green
⊠	3364	◨		260	lt green
Σ	3712			1023	dk rose
■	3750		◨	1036	vy dk blue
•	3021				brown French Knot

The design was stitched over two fabric threads on a 13" x 14" piece of Cream Belfast Linen (32 ct). Two strands of floss were used for Cross Stitch and 1 strand for Backstitch and French Knots. It was custom framed.

Design by Nancy Dockter.

41

This poignant design holds a promising message for a couple beginning a new life together. Featuring a delicate floral border, it makes a thoughtful wedding gift.

Take my hand
And walk with me,
The best in life
Is yet to be.

Linda & Joseph
March 24, 1991

The design was stitched over two fabric threads on a 15" square of Cream Belfast Linen (32 ct). Two strands of floss were used for Cross Stitch and 1 strand for Backstitch and French Knots. It was custom framed.

Design by Mary Scott.

X	DMC	ANC.	COLOR	X	DMC	B'ST	ANC.	COLOR
◎	316	1017	mauve	▲	3726		1018	dk mauve
❖	522	860	green		3768	⁄	779	blue
⊠	927	848	lt blue	•	3768			blue French Knot

109w x 109h

Take my hand
And walk with me,
The best in life
Is yet to be.

center names

center date

43

An innocent offering of flowers from a child is a universal gesture of heartfelt love. Given separately or as a pair, these Amish-inspired designs will be cherished by a devoted mother.

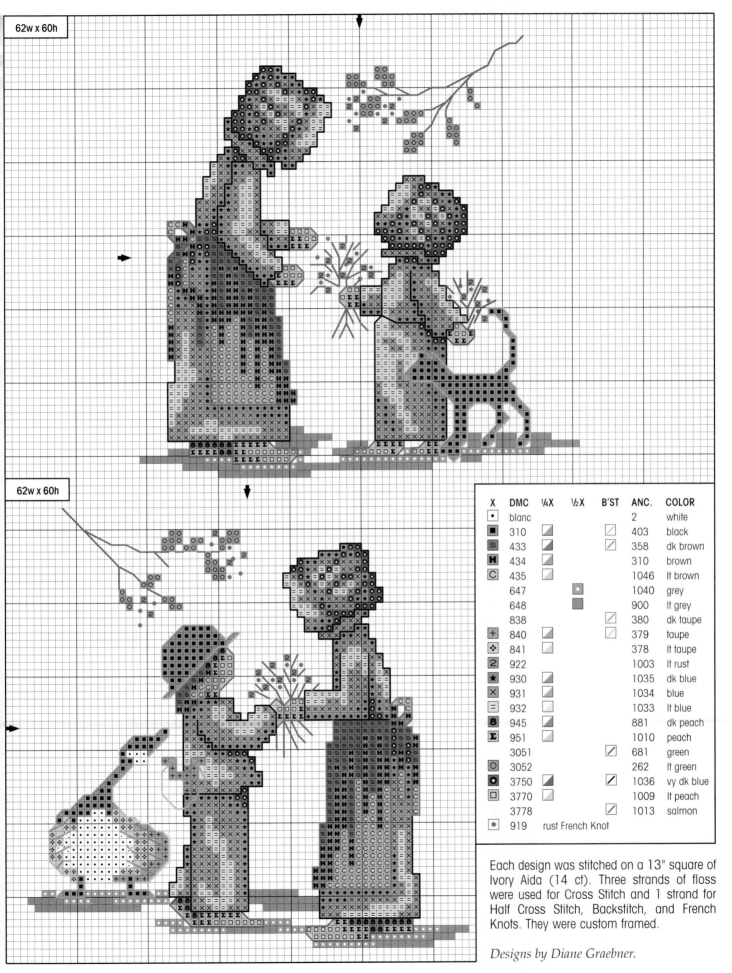

X	DMC	¼X	½X	B'ST	ANC.	COLOR
•	blanc				2	white
■	310	◩		�diag	403	black
S	433	◩		�diag	358	dk brown
H	434	◩			310	brown
C	435	◩			1046	lt brown
	647		▨		1040	grey
	648		▦		900	lt grey
	838			�diag	380	dk taupe
+	840	◩		�diag	379	taupe
❖	841	◩			378	lt taupe
2	922				1003	lt rust
★	930	◩			1035	dk blue
X	931	◩			1034	blue
=	932	◩			1033	lt blue
8	945	◩			881	dk peach
Σ	951	◩			1010	peach
	3051			�diag	681	green
O	3052				262	lt green
✪	3750	◩		�diag	1036	vy dk blue
□	3770	◩			1009	lt peach
	3778			�diag	1013	salmon
•	919	rust French Knot				

Each design was stitched on a 13" square of Ivory Aida (14 ct). Three strands of floss were used for Cross Stitch and 1 strand for Half Cross Stitch, Backstitch, and French Knots. They were custom framed.

Designs by Diane Graebner.

45

Two basic lessons from the Bible are illustrated by these children of yesteryear. How better to represent loving kindness than through a girl and her kitty and a lad with his pup!

LOVE IS OF GOD
I JOHN 4:7

BE YE KIND ONE TO ANOTHER
EPH. 4:32

59w x 88h

50w x 90h

X	DMC	¼X	B'ST	COLOR	X	DMC	¼X	COLOR
•	blanc			white		840		dk beige
	223			dk pink	+	841		beige
	300			dk rust		842		lt beige
	301			lt rust		844		dk grey
	310		/	black		930		dk blue
	400			rust		931		blue
$	433			brown		932		lt blue
X	434			lt brown	=	948		lt peach
	436			tan		3072		lt grey
	471			green		3354		pink
	729			gold		blanc		white French Knot
	754			peach		310		black French Knot
	838			dk brown		838		dk brown French Knot

Each design was stitched on a 12" x 14" piece of Beige Aida (14 ct). Three strands of floss were used for Cross Stitch and 1 strand for Backstitch and French Knots. They were custom framed.

Designs by Camille Harrison.

A marriage of caring and sharing is celebrated with this sweet thought. Quick to stitch, the miniature design is just the right size for a desktop display.

X	DMC	¼X	B'ST	ANC.	COLOR
■	310		∕	403	black
U	415			398	grey
◆	434			310	brown
♡	437			362	tan
◈	553		∕	98	purple
▢	554			96	lt purple
◉	666		∕	46	red
✦	699		∕	923	dk green
▲	701			227	green
☆	703			238	lt green
$	741		∕	304	yellow
✕	744			301	lt yellow
◒	813			161	blue
★	825	◢	∕	162	dk blue
2	828			9159	lt blue
✳	921			1003	rust
✛	948			1011	flesh
⊟	996			433	peacock blue
⊙	825				dk blue French Knot

The design was stitched on a 12" square of Antique White Aida (16 ct). Two strands of floss were used for Cross Stitch and 1 strand for Backstitch and French Knots. It was custom framed.

Design by Kooler Design Studio.

62w x 63h

If good things come in small packages, these simple sayings are the best! The tiny ornaments are so easy that you'll have time to make one for everyone in your family — from an adorable baby to the "World's Greatest Grandpa!"

X	DMC	¼X	B'ST	ANC.	COLOR
•	blanc			2	white
◇	210			108	lt purple
▲	224			893	mauve
	309		╱*	42	rose
	310		╱*	403	black
■	312	◢	╱*	979	dk blue
	317		╱†	400	grey
■	321	◢	╱†	9046	red
✿	334		╱*	977	blue
✳	335	◢	╱*	38	dk pink
U	352			9	coral
▲	436	◢		1045	dk tan
✔	552		╱†	99	dk purple
$	554			96	purple
▽	738			361	tan
∅	739			387	lt tan
+	744			301	yellow
≡	775			128	sky blue
Π	776			24	lt pink
4	780		╱*	310	gold
	838		╱*	380	vy dk taupe
d	839	◢		360	dk taupe
⬟	840			379	taupe
⊠	841			378	lt taupe
8	898			360	brown
◉	930		╱*	1035	grey blue
	938		╱†	381	dk brown
❖	945			881	flesh
H	954			203	green
◣	958	◢	╱	187	dk aqua
O	959			186	aqua
2	964	◢		185	lt aqua
	991		╱*	189	blue green
▷	3325			129	lt blue
☆	3326			36	pink
	3799		╱*	236	dk grey
◉	552				dk purple French Knot
◉	930				grey blue French Knot
◉	938				dk brown French Knot
◉	991				blue green French Knot
◉	3799				dk grey French Knot

* DMC 309 for 2. DMC 310 for 6.
   DMC 312 for 8 and 9.
   DMC 335 for 4 and 10. DMC 838 for 7.
   DMC 930 for 1. DMC 991 for 5.
   DMC 3799 for 3.
† DMC 317 for 8. DMC 321 for 7.
   DMC 552 for 2 and 6. DMC 938 for 4.
★ DMC 334 for 7. DMC 780 for 6.

Each design was stitched on a 6" square of Antique White Aida (18 ct). Two strands of floss were used for Cross Stitch and 1 strand for Backstitch and French Knots. They were inserted in round frames (2½" dia. opening).

Designs by Holly DeFount.

1. 32w x 32h

2. 34w x 31h

3. 30w x 27h

4. 30w x 29h

LIVE
WELL

Simple pleasures are the treasures of life — a friend's warming smile, a fresh-from-the-garden bloom, a stolen moment to daydream. Each little joy buoys our spirits with a refreshing pause from the hectic pace of the day. Included in this uplifting section are scriptures and encouraging thoughts designed to give us a positive perspective. With its optimistic resolution, our One Day at a Time *throw pillow will help you greet the morning with a rosy outlook.*

Design by Lucinda Bruckert.

The design was stitched over two fabric threads on a 17" x 15" piece of New Khaki Lugana (25 ct). Two strands of floss were used for Cross Stitch and 1 strand for Backstitch. It was made into a pillow.

Note: Use a ½" seam allowance for all seams.

For pillow, trim stitched piece 1½" larger than design on all sides. Cut backing fabric same size as stitched piece. Cut one 40" length of ¼" dia. purchased cording with attached seam allowance. Matching raw edges and beginning at bottom edge, pin cording to right side of stitched piece, making a ⅜" clip in seam allowance at each corner. Ends of cording should overlap approximately 4"; turn overlapped ends of cording toward seam allowance and baste across overlapped cording as shown in **Fig. 1**.

For fabric and lace ruffle, match right sides and short edges of a 5" x 70" piece of fabric. Sew short edges together; press seam open. With wrong sides together, match raw edges and press ruffle in half. Sew short edges of a 70" length of 1¾"w flat lace together; press seam open. Matching raw edges of ruffle and straight edge of lace, baste ⅜" and ¼" from raw edge. Pull basting threads, gathering ruffle to fit edge of pillow front. Matching raw edges, pin ruffle to right side of pillow front over cording; baste in place.

Matching right sides and leaving an opening for turning, sew stitched piece and backing fabric together. Trim corners diagonally; turn pillow right side out. Stuff pillow with fiberfill; sew final closure by hand.

X	DMC	¾X	B'ST	ANC.	COLOR
▣	blanc		╱	2	white
☒	223			895	rose
▨	224	◪		893	lt rose
-	225			1026	vy lt rose
	902		╱	897	vy dk rose
◉	3051		╱	681	dk green
◈	3052			262	green
▢	3053			261	lt green
★	3721	◪	╱	896	dk rose

Fig. 1

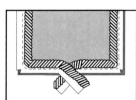

Even fairy-tale wishes can come true — if you believe! Graced with the magic of a mystical unicorn, this little design encourages us to follow our dreams.

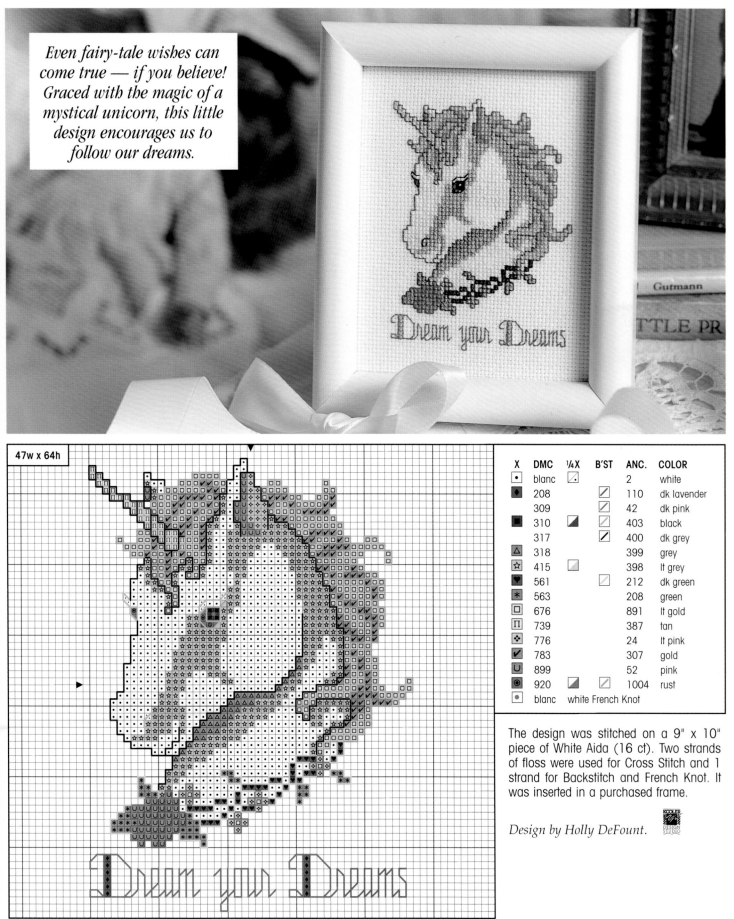

47w x 64h

X	DMC	¼X	B'ST	ANC.	COLOR
•	blanc	⟋		2	white
◆	208		⟋	110	dk lavender
	309		⟋	42	dk pink
■	310	◢	⟋	403	black
	317		⟋	400	dk grey
△	318			399	grey
☆	415	⟋		398	lt grey
♥	561		⟋	212	dk green
✳	563			208	green
☐	676			891	lt gold
Π	739			387	tan
✦	776			24	lt pink
✔	783			307	gold
U	899			52	pink
◉	920	◢	⟋	1004	rust
⦿	blanc		white French Knot		

The design was stitched on a 9" x 10" piece of White Aida (16 ct). Two strands of floss were used for Cross Stitch and 1 strand for Backstitch and French Knot. It was inserted in a purchased frame.

Design by Holly DeFount.

These sunny bookmarks make inexpensive, inspirational gifts for anyone who's close to your heart. Slip one into a letter or birthday card to brighten the day of a friend who lives far away.

ASHLEY'S BOOK

Do You Need Proof of God ? Does One Light a Torch to see the Sun

Follow your dreams

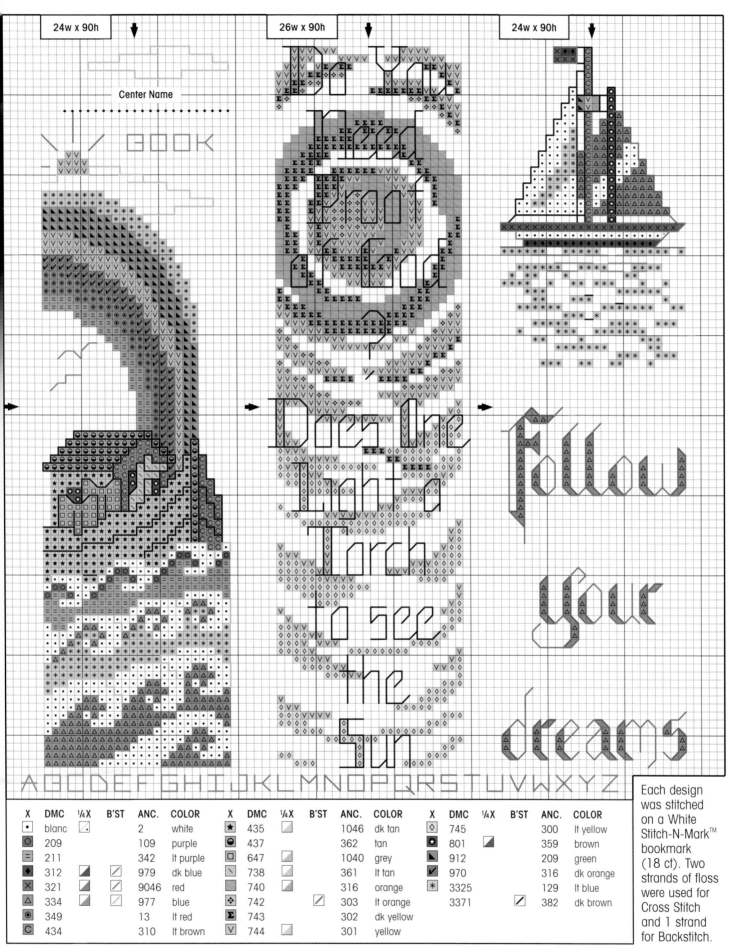

X	DMC	1/4 X	B'ST	ANC.	COLOR		X	DMC	1/4 X	B'ST	ANC.	COLOR		X	DMC	1/4 X	B'ST	ANC.	COLOR
•	blanc			2	white		★	435			1046	dk tan		◇	745			300	lt yellow
◉	209			109	purple		◒	437			362	tan		✿	801			359	brown
=	211			342	lt purple		▢	647			1040	grey		◣	912			209	green
◆	312	◪	◿	979	dk blue		◣	738			361	lt tan		✔	970			316	dk orange
✕	321	◪	◿	9046	red			740			316	orange		✳	3325			129	lt blue
△	334	◪	◿	977	blue		✤	742		◿	303	lt orange			3371		◿	382	dk brown
◉	349			13	lt red		Σ	743			302	dk yellow							
C	434			310	lt brown		V	744	◹		301	yellow							

Designs by Terrie Lee Steinmeyer © 1992.

Each design was stitched on a White Stitch-N-Mark™ bookmark (18 ct). Two strands of floss were used for Cross Stitch and 1 strand for Backstitch.

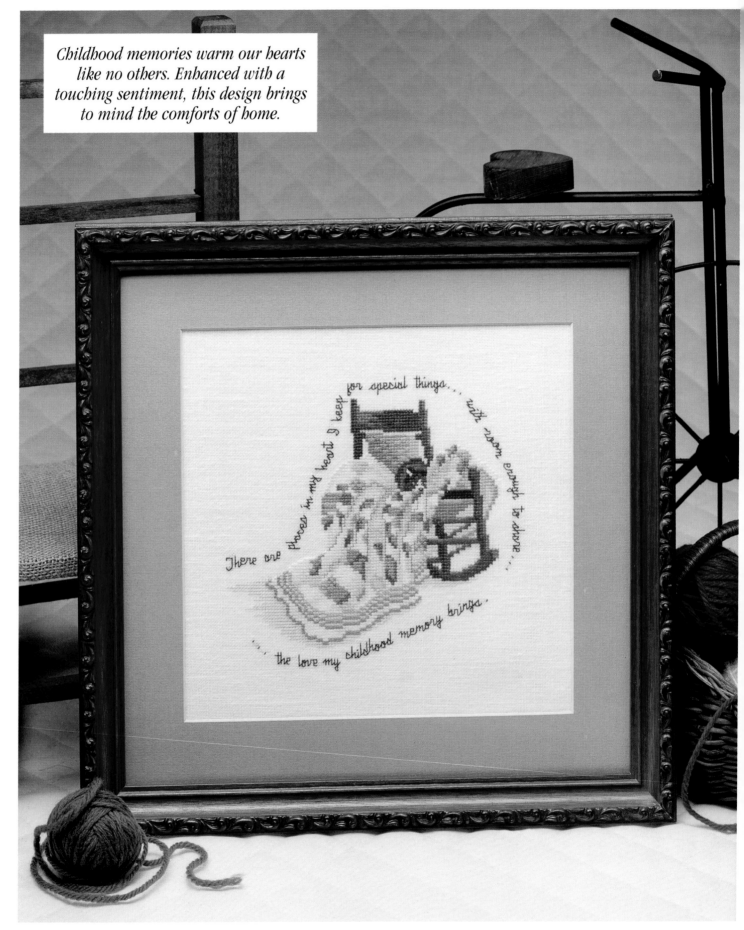

Childhood memories warm our hearts like no others. Enhanced with a touching sentiment, this design brings to mind the comforts of home.

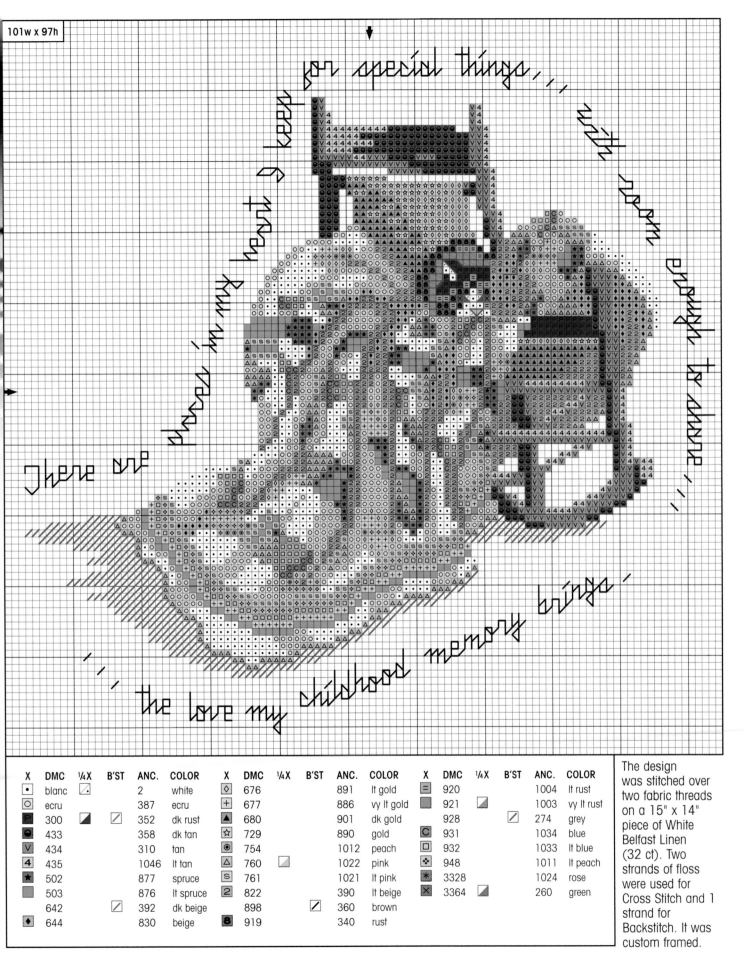

X	DMC	¼X	B'ST	ANC.	COLOR	X	DMC	¼X	B'ST	ANC.	COLOR	X	DMC	¼X	B'ST	ANC.	COLOR
•	blanc			2	white	◇	676			891	lt gold	=	920			1004	lt rust
○	ecru			387	ecru	+	677			886	vy lt gold		921			1003	vy lt rust
	300			352	dk rust	▲	680			901	dk gold		928			274	grey
	433			358	dk tan	☆	729			890	gold	C	931			1034	blue
V	434			310	tan	◉	754			1012	peach	□	932			1033	lt blue
4	435			1046	lt tan	△	760			1022	pink	✿	948			1011	lt peach
★	502			877	spruce	S	761			1021	lt pink	✳	3328			1024	rose
	503			876	lt spruce	2	822			390	lt beige	✕	3364			260	green
	642			392	dk beige		898			360	brown						
◆	644			830	beige	8	919			340	rust						

The design was stitched over two fabric threads on a 15" x 14" piece of White Belfast Linen (32 ct). Two strands of floss were used for Cross Stitch and 1 strand for Backstitch. It was custom framed.

Design adapted from original artwork by Doris Morgan.

Share the warmth of a cup of tea that's sweetened with words of encouragement. Our mug designs offer a delightful break-time boost for friends.

60

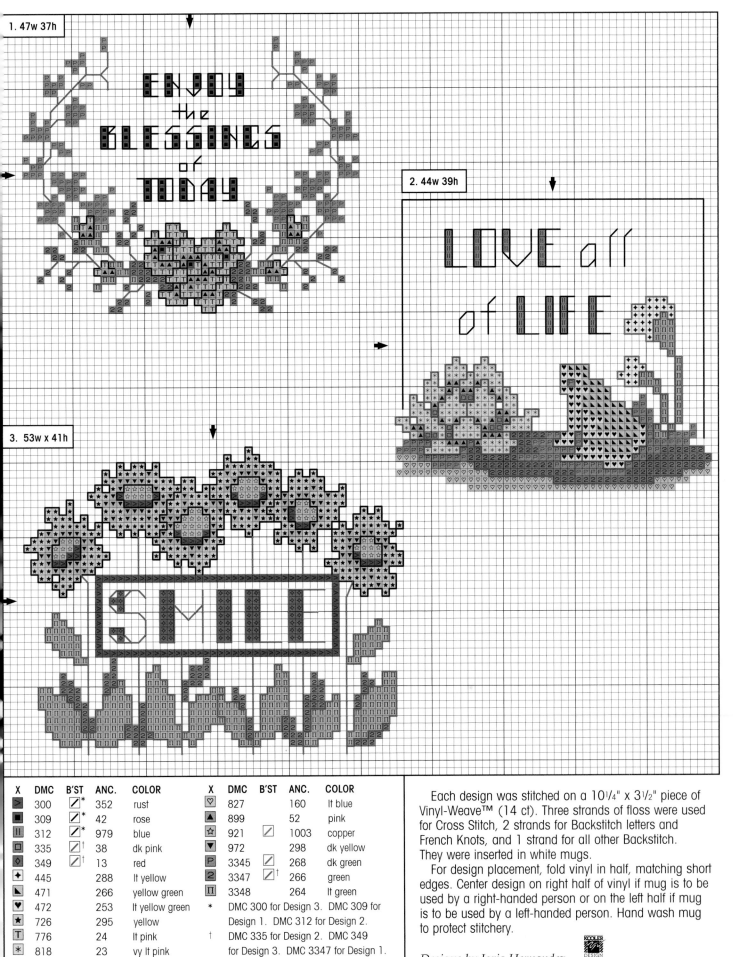

1. 47w 37h

ENJOY the BLESSINGS of TODAY

2. 44w 39h

LOVE all of LIFE

3. 53w x 41h

SMILE

X	DMC	B'ST	ANC.	COLOR	X	DMC	B'ST	ANC.	COLOR
>	300	⟋*	352	rust	♡	827		160	lt blue
■	309	⟋*	42	rose	▲	899		52	pink
‖	312	⟋*	979	blue	☆	921	⟋	1003	copper
□	335	⟋†	38	dk pink	▼	972		298	dk yellow
◇	349	⟋†	13	red	P	3345	⟋	268	dk green
✦	445		288	lt yellow	2	3347	⟋†	266	green
◣	471		266	yellow green	Π	3348		264	lt green
♥	472		253	lt yellow green	*	DMC 300 for Design 3. DMC 309 for			
★	726		295	yellow		Design 1. DMC 312 for Design 2.			
T	776		24	lt pink	†	DMC 335 for Design 2. DMC 349			
✳	818		23	vy lt pink		for Design 3. DMC 3347 for Design 1.			

Each design was stitched on a 10¼" x 3½" piece of Vinyl-Weave™ (14 ct). Three strands of floss were used for Cross Stitch, 2 strands for Backstitch letters and French Knots, and 1 strand for all other Backstitch. They were inserted in white mugs.

For design placement, fold vinyl in half, matching short edges. Center design on right half of vinyl if mug is to be used by a right-handed person or on the left half if mug is to be used by a left-handed person. Hand wash mug to protect stitchery.

Designs by Jorja Hernandez.

*Into every life, a little rain
must fall, so the saying goes.
But those dark clouds are
soon replaced with a
glorious rainbow — and its
promise of new beginnings.*

X	DMC	¼X	B'ST	ANC.	COLOR
•	blanc			2	white
♥	210			108	lavender
T	211			342	lt lavender
*	434			310	lt brown
▽	436			1045	dk tan
U	437			362	tan
◯	632			936	rose brown
%	646			8581	dk grey
V	647			1040	grey
◯	648			900	lt grey
◻	712			926	cream
◉	744			301	dk yellow
+	745			300	yellow
✕	746			275	lt yellow
☆	776			24	lt pink
	801		◸	359	brown
	898		◸	360	dk brown
▲	899			52	pink
4	948			1011	flesh
♥	954			203	green
✦	955			206	lt green
◇	3032			903	dk beige
✕	3325			129	lt blue
2	3755			140	blue
⊟	3772			1007	lt rose brown
◣	3782			899	beige
▦	3799		◸	236	charcoal grey
◉	801	brown French Knot			

41w x 58h

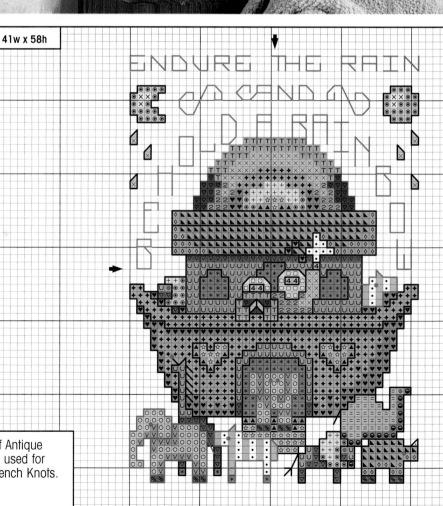

The design was stitched on a 9" x 10" piece of Antique
White Aida (14 ct). Three strands of floss were used for
Cross Stitch and 1 strand for Backstitch and French Knots.
It was inserted in a purchased peg frame.

Design by Deborah Lambein.

This little verse reminds us that even the smallest efforts can bring great rewards if we've done our best. Quick to stitch, the design is a thoughtful pick-me-up gift.

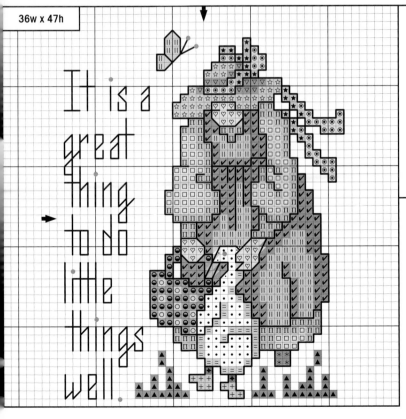

36w x 47h

X	DMC	¼X	COLOR	X	DMC	¼X	B'ST	COLOR
•	blanc		white	□	745			lt yellow
▲	320		green	○	754			flesh
★	352		peach		801		/	dk brown
◉	353		lt peach	=	822			beige
◒	356		rust	✦	922			copper
+	402		lt copper	♡	948			lt flesh
✳	434		brown	‖	3325			lt blue
▽	436		lt brown	✔	3755			blue
☆	738		tan	•	801		dk brown French Knot	
Π	743		yellow					

The design was stitched on a 9" x 10" piece of Antique White Aida (14 ct). Three strands of floss were used for Cross Stitch and 1 strand for Backstitch and French Knots. It was inserted in a purchased frame.

Design by Deborah Lambein.

This bold sunflower evokes the warmth of long summer days. It will brighten a corner of your home or bring lasting sunshine to a gardening friend.

74w x 107h

X	DMC	B'ST	COLOR
△	433		brown
◇	434		lt brown
◕	469		dk green
✳	470		green
◉	471		lt green
☆	472		vy lt green
○	725		yellow
+	727		lt yellow
★	782		gold
□	783		lt gold
◆	898		dk brown
▲	935	╱	vy dk green
	975	╱	rust
■	3371		brown black

The design was stitched over two fabric threads on a 14" x 17" piece of Cream Lugana (25 ct). Three strands of floss were used for Cross Stitch and 1 strand for Backstitch. It was custom framed.

Design by Lou Anne Blakely.

Accented with darling motifs, these perky kitchen towels will warm the heart of any home. Choose flowers, watermelons, or a teddy bear to add a welcoming touch to cheery checked towels.

WELCOME

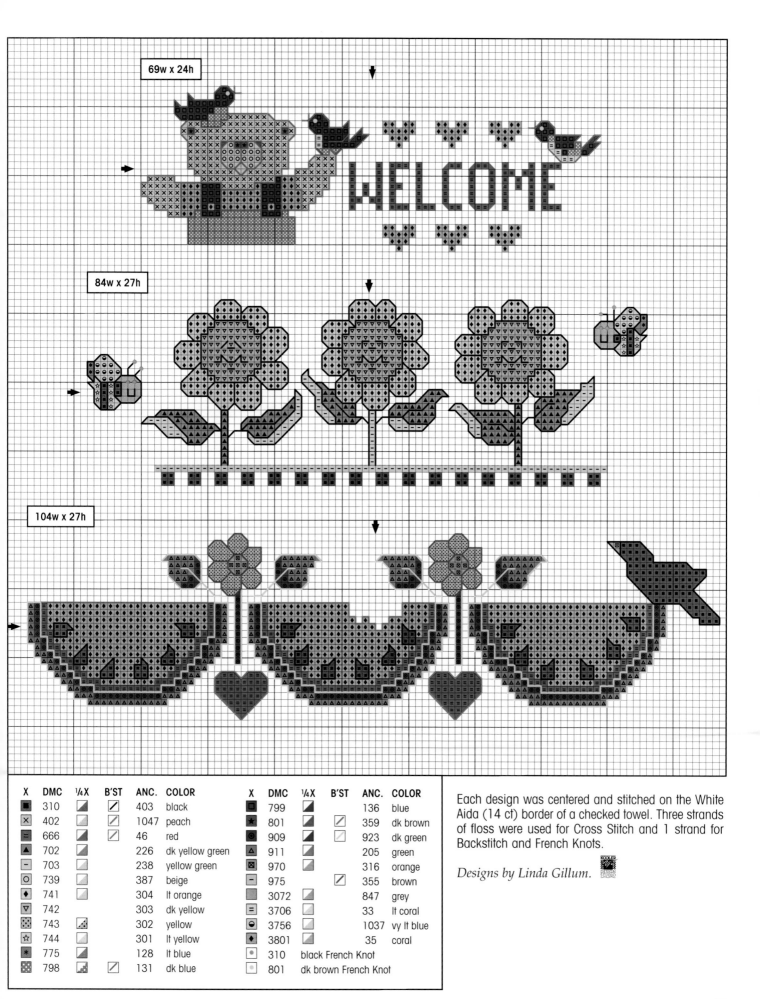

X	DMC	¼X	B'ST	ANC.	COLOR		X	DMC	¼X	B'ST	ANC.	COLOR
■	310	◪	⁄	403	black		■	799	◪		136	blue
×	402	◪	⁄	1047	peach		★	801	◪	⁄	359	dk brown
≡	666	◪	⁄	46	red		◉	909	◪	⁄	923	dk green
▲	702	◪		226	dk yellow green		△	911	◪		205	green
-	703	◪		238	yellow green		⊠	970	◪		316	orange
○	739	◪		387	beige		-	975	◪	⁄	355	brown
◆	741	◪		304	lt orange			3072	◪		847	grey
▽	742	◪		303	dk yellow		=	3706	◪		33	lt coral
⊡	743	◪		302	yellow		⊖	3756	◪		1037	vy lt blue
☆	744	◪		301	lt yellow		◆	3801	◪		35	coral
∗	775	◪		128	lt blue		·	310				black French Knot
▦	798	◪	⁄	131	dk blue		○	801				dk brown French Knot

Each design was centered and stitched on the White Aida (14 ct) border of a checked towel. Three strands of floss were used for Cross Stitch and 1 strand for Backstitch and French Knots.

Designs by Linda Gillum.

Nestled beneath a starry winter sky, a cozy cabin beams with warmth. The reflective verse beckons us to enjoy the closeness of family and friends.

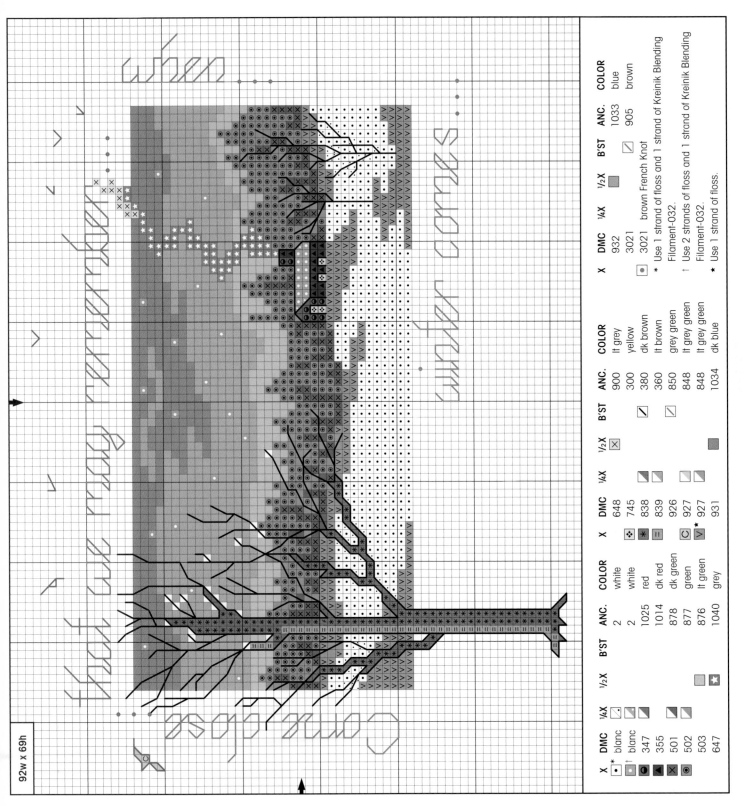

92w x 69h

X	¼X	½X	B'ST	ANC.	DMC	COLOR
				2	blanc	white
				2	blanc	white
				1025	347	red
				1014	355	dk red
				878	501	dk green
				877	502	green
				876	503	lt green
				1040	647	grey

X	¼X	½X	B'ST	ANC.	DMC	COLOR
				900	648	lt grey
				300	745	yellow
				380	838	dk brown
				360	839	lt brown
				850	926	grey green
				848	927	lt grey green
				848	927	lt grey green
				1034	931	dk blue

X	¼X	½X	B'ST	ANC.	DMC	COLOR
				1033	932	blue
				905	3021	brown
					3021	brown French Knot

* Use 1 strand of floss and 1 strand of Kreinik Blending Filament-032.

† Use 2 strands of floss and 1 strand of Kreinik Blending Filament-032.

★ Use 1 strand of floss.

The design was stitched over two fabric threads on a 14" x 13" piece of Antique White Belfast Linen (32 ct). Two strands of floss were used for Cross Stitch and 1 strand for Half Cross Stitch, Backstitch, and French Knots unless otherwise noted in color key. It was custom framed.

Design by Doris Morgan.
Needlework adaptation by Linda Culp Calhoun.

This sunny design is sure to chase away gloomy days! Stitched in vibrant colors, it's a chipper reminder to leave those worries behind.

The design was stitched on a 17" x 10" piece of Antique White Aida (14 ct). Three strands of floss were used for Cross Stitch and 1 strand for Backstitch and French Knots. It was custom framed.

Design by Linda Gillum.

123w x 28h

X	¼X	B'ST	DMC	ANC.	COLOR
●			208	110	purple
2			312	979	blue
✚			321	9046	red
■			740	9046	red
❖			742	316	orange
◆		╱	743	303	dk yellow
◑			745	302	yellow
◐			838	300	lt yellow
✕		╱	910	380	brown
‖		╱	922	229	green
▼	◤	╱	1003	1003	lt rust
			321		red French Knot

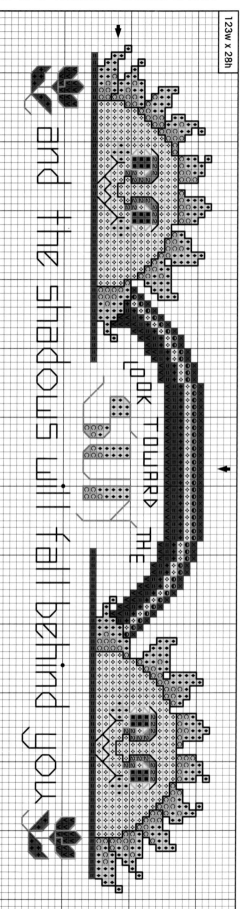

STITCHERS COUNT!

This simple sampler declares a sentiment that we've always shared — stitchers are people who count! The quick-and-easy design is perfect for beginners or a last-minute gift.

47w x 54h

X	DMC	¼X	B'ST	ANC.	COLOR
✕	312	◢	✓	979	dk blue
○	334	◢		977	blue
✳	666	◢	✓	46	red
▼	911		✓	205	green
=	3325	☐		129	lt blue

The design was stitched on a 9" x 10" piece of Antique White Aida (16 ct). Two strands of floss were used for Cross Stitch and 1 strand for Backstitch. It was inserted in a purchased frame (5" square opening).

Design by Kooler Design Studio.

Noting the calming effects of a pretty melody, this design sets the tone for musical moments. The piece is especially soothing when accompanied by the soulful sounds of your favorite tunes.

65w x 99h

X	DMC	1/4X	B'ST	ANC.
•	blanc			2
■	310		∕	403
★	321		∕	9046
✳	322	◢	∕	978
◆	743			302
○	744			301
+	745			300
	782		∕	308
◉	899			52
●	910		∕	229
▽	912			209
☆	954			203
▢	3325			129

The design was stitched on a 13" x 15" piece of White Aida (14 ct). Three strands of floss were used for Cross Stitch and 1 strand for Backstitch. It was custom framed.

Design by Linda Gillum.

73

Fresh from the garden, these clever thoughts offer a bounty of sage advice. The easy miniatures are great for quick gifts by themselves or as clever package tie-ons.

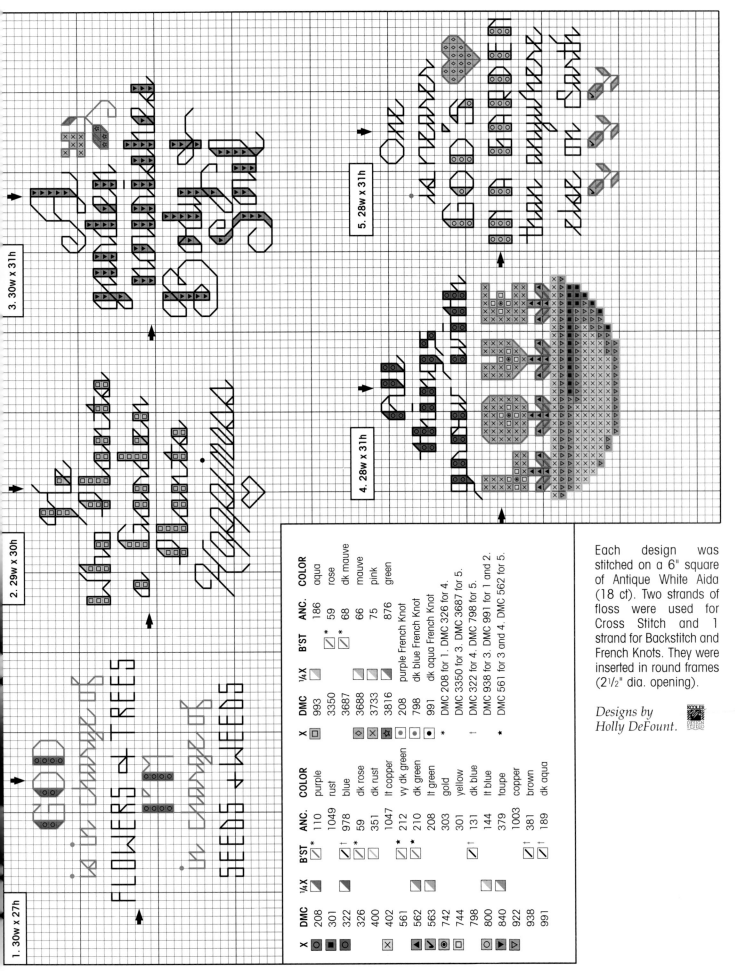

Each design was stitched on a 6" square of Antique White Aida (18 ct). Two strands of floss were used for Cross Stitch and 1 strand for Backstitch and French Knots. They were inserted in round frames (2½" dia. opening).

Designs by Holly DeFount.

DMC	¼X	B'ST	ANC.	COLOR
208		*	110	purple
301		†	1049	rust
322		*	978	blue
326			59	dk rose
400			351	dk rust
402			1047	lt copper
561		★	212	vy dk green
562		★	210	dk green
563			208	lt green
742			303	gold
744			301	yellow
798		†	131	dk blue
800			144	lt blue
840			379	taupe
922			1003	copper
938		†	381	brown
991		†	189	dk aqua

X	¼X	B'ST	ANC.	COLOR
993			186	aqua
3350		*	59	rose
3687		*	68	dk mauve
3688			66	mauve
3733			75	pink
3816			876	green
208				purple French Knot
798				dk blue French Knot
991				dk aqua French Knot

* DMC 208 for 1. DMC 326 for 4.
* DMC 3350 for 3. DMC 3687 for 5.
† DMC 322 for 4. DMC 798 for 5.
★ DMC 938 for 3. DMC 991 for 1 and 2.
★ DMC 561 for 3 and 4. DMC 562 for 5.

1. 30w x 27h

2. 29w x 30h

3. 30w x 31h

4. 28w x 31h

5. 28w x 31h

No matter how many miles may separate them, true friends are always near at heart. This simple treasure is a tender way to share that sentiment with far-away loved ones.

X	DMC	¼X	B'ST	ANC.	COLOR
•	blanc			2	white
◉	318			399	grey
★	320			215	green
◕	347			1025	red
	413		╱	401	dk grey
+	415			398	lt grey
✳	433	◢		358	brown
◆	921	◢		1003	rust
△	932	◢		1033	blue
⊙	413		dk grey French Knot

The design was stitched on a 10" square of Fiddler's Lite® (14 ct). Three strands of floss were used for Cross Stitch and 1 strand for Backstitch and French Knots. It was inserted in a purchased frame.

Design by Holly DeFount.

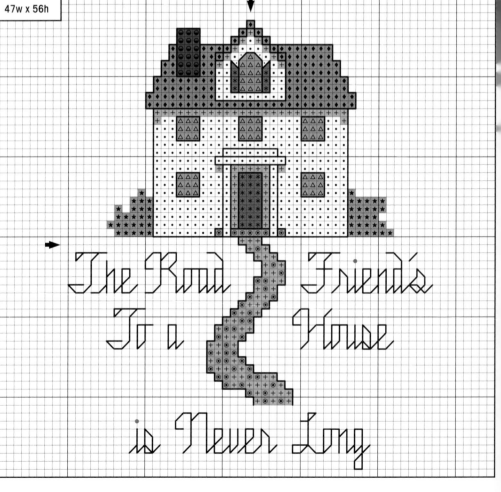

OUR DAILY BREAD

Stitched on a fringed bread cloth, a familiar verse from the Bible reminds us to give thanks for the blessings we enjoy every day.

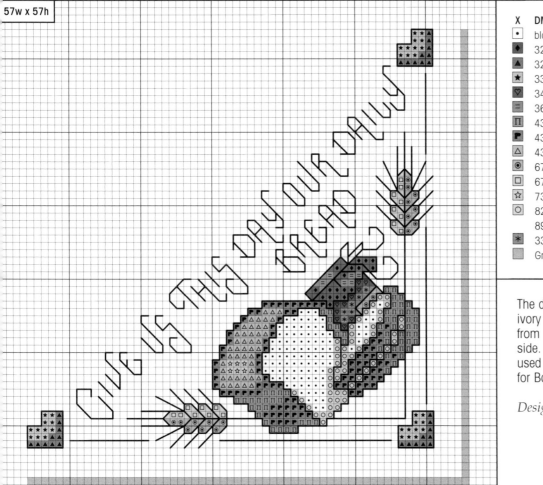

57w x 57h

X	DMC	¼X	B'ST	ANC.	COLOR
·	blanc			2	white
♦	320	◨		215	green
▲	322	·		978	blue
★	334			977	lt blue
♡	347	◨		1025	red
=	368	◨		214	lt green
Π	434			310	lt brown
▣	436			1045	dk tan
△	437			362	tan
◉	676	◨		891	gold
☐	677	◨		886	lt gold
☆	738			361	lt tan
○	822			390	beige
	898		◿	360	brown
✳	3328	◨		1024	lt red
▥	Grey area indicates beginning of fringe.				

The design was stitched on an ivory bread cover (14 ct), 4 squares from beginning of fringe on each side. Three strands of floss were used for Cross Stitch and 1 strand for Backstitch.

Design by Deborah Lambein.

Bring blessings to your table all year long with a collection of bread cloths. Carrying baskets to gather the bounty of each season, these angels will help you celebrate four special harvests.

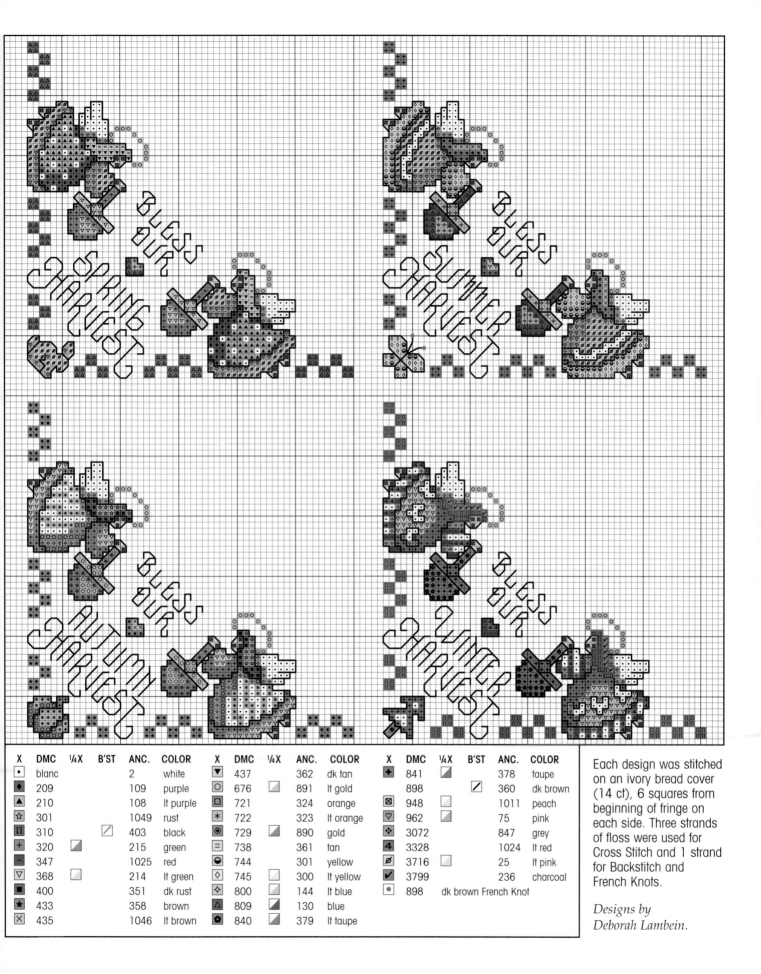

X	DMC	¼X	B'ST	ANC.	COLOR	X	DMC	¼X	ANC.	COLOR	X	DMC	¼X	B'ST	ANC.	COLOR
•	blanc			2	white	▼	437		362	dk tan	✦	841			378	taupe
◆	209			109	purple	○	676		891	lt gold		898		／	360	dk brown
▲	210			108	lt purple	▢	721		324	orange	⊠	948			1011	peach
☆	301			1049	rust	✳	722		323	lt orange	▽	962			75	pink
⊓	310		／	403	black	◉	729		890	gold	✧	3072			847	grey
✛	320			215	green	＝	738		361	tan	4	3328			1024	lt red
▬	347			1025	red	◖	744		301	yellow	⌀	3716			25	lt pink
▽	368			214	lt green	◇	745		300	lt yellow	✔	3799			236	charcoal
■	400			351	dk rust	✧	800		144	lt blue	⊙	898				dk brown French Knot
★	433			358	brown	△	809		130	blue						
⊠	435			1046	lt brown	⬠	840		379	lt taupe						

Each design was stitched on an ivory bread cover (14 ct), 6 squares from beginning of fringe on each side. Three strands of floss were used for Cross Stitch and 1 strand for Backstitch and French Knots.

Designs by
Deborah Lambein.

No matter what the day may bring, we can always find a reason to rejoice. After all, every day is a generous gift from God!

98w x 98h

the Lord has made. Let us

This is the day which

rejoice and be glad in it

Psalms 118:24

X	DMC	1/4X	1/2X	B'ST	ANC.	COLOR		X	DMC	1/4X	1/2X	B'ST	ANC.	COLOR
•	blanc				2	white		★	839				360	dk taupe
♡	223				895	lt rose		✕	840				379	taupe
■	310				403	black		▲	844				1041	grey black
	320				215	lt green		5	926				850	blue grey
	367				217	green		◖	927				848	lt blue grey
Σ	434				310	brown			930				1035	blue
4	435				1046	lt brown		=	932				1033	lt blue
C	501				878	blue green		◇	948				1011	lt peach
☆	502				877	lt blue green			3041				871	mauve
◉	725				305	dk yellow			3042				870	lt mauve
V	726				295	yellow		*	3072				847	grey
O	745				300	lt yellow		P	3721				896	dk rose
V	754				1012	peach		Π	3722				1027	rose
❖	761				1021	pink		◉	310					black French Knot

The design was stitched over two fabric threads on a 14" square of Cream Belfast Linen (32 ct). Two strands of floss were used for Cross Stitch and 1 strand for Half Cross Stitch, Backstitch, and French Knots. It was custom framed.

Design by Debbie Kingston.

These thoughtful verses inspire us to make our homes havens of love for our families.

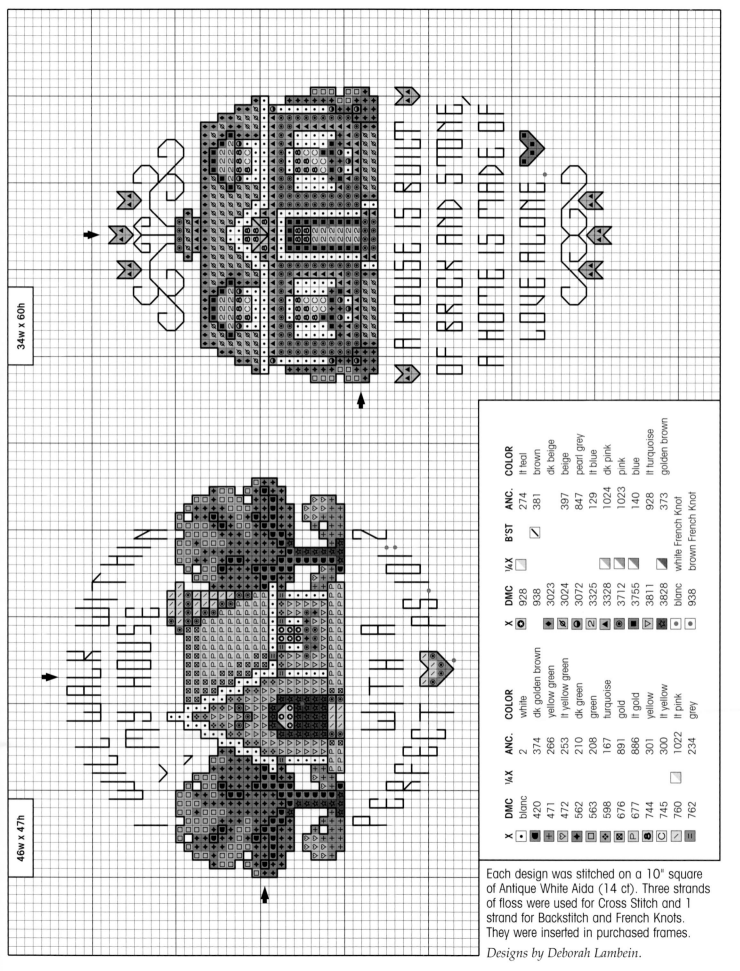

34w x 60h

A HOUSE IS BUILT OF BRICK AND STONE,

A HOME IS MADE OF LOVE ALONE

46w x 47h

WALK WITHIN

THIS HOUSE

PERFECT PEACE WITH US

X	DMC	¼X	ANC.	COLOR
•	blanc		2	white
■	420		374	dk golden brown
+	471		266	yellow green
▷	472		253	lt yellow green
✦	562		210	dk green
☐	563		208	green
✤	598		167	turquoise
⊠	676		891	gold
P	677		886	lt gold
⊗	744		301	yellow
C	745		300	lt yellow
╱	760	◱	1022	lt pink
‖	762		234	grey

X	DMC	¼X	B'ST	ANC.	COLOR
✿	928	◱	╲	274	lt teal
◆	938			381	brown
⊘	3023				dk beige
◐	3024			397	beige
2	3072			847	pearl grey
◀	3325			129	lt blue
◉	3328	◱		1024	dk pink
■	3712	◱		1023	pink
▷	3755	◱		140	blue
☆	3811	◣		928	lt turquoise
• •	3828			373	golden brown
•	blanc				white French Knot
•	938				brown French Knot

Each design was stitched on a 10" square of Antique White Aida (14 ct). Three strands of floss were used for Cross Stitch and 1 strand for Backstitch and French Knots. They were inserted in purchased frames.

Designs by Deborah Lambein.

With her patched wings and worn
sweater, this charming angel conveys a
message of faith in God's divine plan.

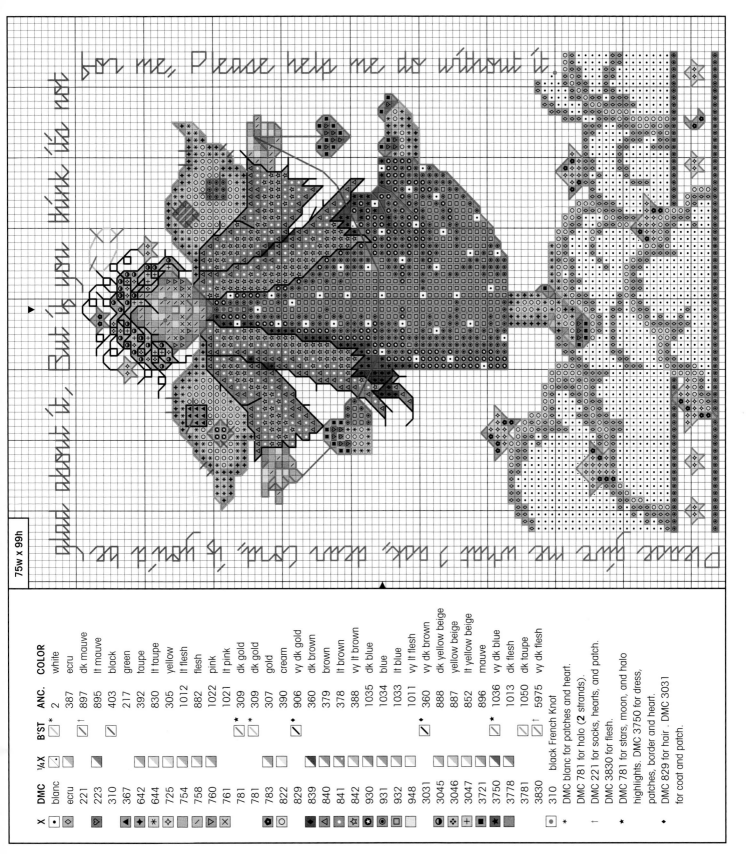

X	DMC	1/4X	B'ST	ANC.	COLOR
	blanc			2	white
	ecru			387	ecru
	221			897	dk mauve
	223			895	lt mauve
	310			403	black
	367			217	green
	642			392	toupe
	644			830	lt taupe
	725			305	yellow
	754			1012	lt flesh
	758			882	flesh
	760			1022	pink
	761			1021	lt pink
	781			309	dk gold
	781			309	dk gold
	783			307	gold
	822			390	cream
	829			906	vy dk gold
	839			360	dk brown
	840			379	brown
	841			378	lt brown
	842			388	vy lt brown
	930			1035	dk blue
	931			1034	blue
	932			1033	lt blue
	948			1011	vy lt flesh
	3031			360	vy dk brown
	3045			888	dk yellow beige
	3046			887	yellow beige
	3047			852	lt yellow beige
	3721			896	mauve
	3750			1036	vy dk blue
	3778			1013	dk flesh
	3781			1050	dk taupe
	3830			5975	vy dk flesh
	310				black French Knot

DMC blanc for patches and heart.
DMC 781 for halo (2 strands).
DMC 221 for socks, hearts, and patch.
DMC 3830 for flesh.
DMC 781 for stars, moon, and halo highlights. DMC 3750 for dress, patches, border and heart.
DMC 829 for hair. DMC 3031 for coat and patch.

75w x 99h

The design was stitched over two fabric threads on a 14" x 16" piece of Antique White Lugana (25 ct). Three strands of floss were used for Cross Stitch and 1 strand for Backstitch and French Knots unless otherwise noted in color key. It was custom framed.

Design by Sandi Gore Evans.

A little one will drift away to peaceful dreams beneath this sweet verse. The proverb is accented with a "beary" cute pair of teddies napping on cottony clouds.

84w x 56h

The design was stitched on a 14" x 12" piece of White Aida (14 ct). Three strands of floss were used for Cross Stitch and 1 strand for Backstitch and French Knots unless otherwise noted in color key. It was custom framed.

Design by Lorri Birmingham.

X	DMC	1/4X	B'ST	ANC.	COLOR	X	DMC	1/4X	B'ST	ANC.	COLOR	X	DMC	1/4X	ANC.	COLOR
•	blanc			2	white	Σ	744	✓		301	yellow	♡	963	✓	73	lt pink
◉	210	✓		108	purple	5	761			1021	salmon	◁	3325		129	lt blue
◇	211			342	lt purple	%	775	✓		128	vy lt blue	✕	3716	✓	25	pink
	334	✓		977	dk blue		783		✓	307	gold	★	3755		140	blue
◆	353			6	lt peach		898		✓	360	brown	✔	3823	✓	386	lt yellow
◢	436	✓		1045	dk tan		898		✓ *	360	brown	+	3824	✓	8	peach
○	437	✓		362	tan	8	954	✓		203	green	●	334			dk blue French Knot
＼	738	✓		361	lt tan	□	955			206	lt green	●	783			gold french Knot
＝	739	✓		387	vy lt tan	▽	962	✓		75	dk pink	*	Use 6 strands for bears' eyes.			

Tiny bluebirds illustrate a loving lesson for all of us — the more friends who come calling, the merrier our homes will be! For a cheerful presentation, affix the framed piece to a twig wreath embellished with ornaments from nature.

42w x 53h

X	DMC	¼X	B'ST	ANC.	COLOR
•	blanc			2	white
■	310	◪	◪	403	black
★	434			310	lt brown
▽	436			1045	tan
◖	562			210	dk green
✦	563			208	green
✕	564			206	lt green
▲	744	◪		301	yellow
$	745			300	lt yellow
✳	762			234	lt grey
▽	775	◪		128	lt blue
+	776	◪		24	lt pink
✖	899			52	dk pink
	938		◪	381	brown
♥	3325	◪		129	blue
◉	3326			36	pink
2	3799	◪		236	grey
◉	938	brown French Knot			

The design was stitched on a 9" x 10" piece of Antique White Aida (14 ct). Three strands of floss were used for Cross Stitch and 1 strand for Backstitch and French Knots. It was inserted in a purchased frame and attached to a wreath.

Design by Deborah Lambein.

Providing comfort for the soul as well as the body, this beautiful pillow bears words that convey warmth and contentment.

strawberries·sunshine
prayers·laughter·music
hope·quiet·love·tears
children·rainbows

X	DMC	B'ST	ANC.	COLOR
V	320		215	lt green
	367	/	217	green
	543		933	tan
	930	/	1035	blue
O	3722	/	1027	pink
•	930			blue French Knot
●	3722			pink French Knot

The design was stitched over two fabric threads on a 15" x 13" piece of Antique White Lugana (25 ct). Three strands of floss were used for Cross Stitch and 1 strand for Backstitch and French Knots. It was made into a pillow.

Note: Use a 1/2" seam allowance for all seams.

For pillow, trim stitched piece 1" larger than design on all sides. Cut a piece of fabric same size as stitched piece for lining. Baste lining fabric to back of stitched piece close to raw edges.

For cording, cut one 30" length of 1/4" dia. cording with attached seam allowance. Matching raw edges and beginning at center bottom, pin cording to right side of stitched piece. Overlap ends of cording and tack in place; trim excess cording. Using zipper foot, baste cording in place. Press seam allowances toward wrong side of stitched piece.

For pillow front and back, cut two 14" x 12¼" pieces of fabric. Center stitched piece right side up on right side of one piece of fabric; pin in place. Using zipper foot and thread to match cording, attach stitched piece

to pillow front, sewing as close as possible to cording, taking care not to catch fabric of stitched piece.

Cut a 54" length of 1½"w fringe. Matching raw edge of pillow front and bound edge of fringe, pin fringe to right side of pillow front. Trim ends of fringe to meet exactly. Sew fringe to pillow front. Matching right sides and leaving an opening for turning, sew pillow front and back together. Trim corners diagonally; turn pillow right side out. Stuff pillow with fiberfill; sew final closure by hand.

Design by Pam McKee.
Needlework adaptation by Jane Chandler.

Stitched in soft, soothing colors, a traditional quilt block design is enhanced with pastel hearts. The nostalgic verse provides a moment of quiet contemplation.

We keep in our hearts our fancies and dreams

We never really grow old it seems

And in a corner all tucked away

To the child we all were yesterday.

X	DMC	B'ST	ANC.	COLOR
	315	/	1019	dk pink
V	316	/	1017	pink
	501	/	878	green
+	778		968	lt pink
	924	/	851	dk blue
X	926	/	850	blue
S	927		848	lt blue
•	924			dk blue French Knot
•	926			blue French Knot
Ø	501			green Lazy Daisy Stitch

The design was stitched over two fabric threads on a 16" square of Bone Lugana (25 ct). Three strands of floss were used for Cross Stitch and 1 strand for Backstitch, French Knots, and Lazy Daisy Stitches. It was custom framed.

Design by Pam McKee.

Bordered with delicate flowers, this design is perfect for celebrating the coming of spring or welcoming guests into your home.

108w x 47h

X	DMC	ANC.	COLOR	1/4X	B'ST
·	blanc	2	white		
	209	109	dk purple	◪	◪
	210	108	purple	◪	
	211	342	lt purple	◪	
	312	979	navy	◪	◪
	322	978	vy lt navy	◪	◪
	334	977	dk navy	◪	
	336	150	dk navy	◪	◪
	347	1025	red	◪	
	367	217	green	◪	
	434	310	vy dk gold	◪	

X	DMC	ANC.	COLOR	1/4X	B'ST
	500	683	dk grey green	◪	◪
	501	878	grey green	◪	
	502	877	lt grey green	◪	
	676	891	gold	◪	
	677	886	lt gold	◪	
	680	901	dk gold	◪	◪
	720	326	orange	◪	
	743	302	yellow	◪	
	744	301	lt yellow	◪	
	760	1022	salmon	◪	
	761	1021	lt salmon	◪	

X	DMC	ANC.	COLOR	1/4X	B'ST
S	813	161	lt blue	◪	◪
☆	816	1005	dk red	◪	◪
	825	162	dk blue	◪	◪
P	826	161	blue		
⊘	844	1041	brown grey		
	3325	129	vy lt blue	◪	
8	3328	1024	lt red	◪	◪
·	3345	268	yellow green	◪	
	3347	266	lt yellow green		
	434		vy dk gold French Knot		

The design was stitched over two fabric threads on a 15" x 11" piece of Cream Belfast Linen (32 ct). Two strands of floss were used for Cross Stitch and 1 strand for Backstitch and French Knots. It was custom framed.

Design by Nancy Dockter.

93

This heartfelt prayer, framed with dainty blossoms, reflects the desire that every one of us has for the health and happiness of our family.

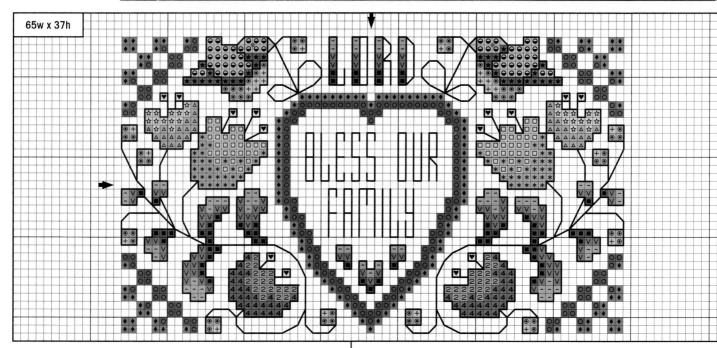

65w x 37h

The design was stitched on an 11" x 9" piece of Antique White Aida (14 ct). Three strands of floss were used for Cross Stitch and 1 strand for Backstitch and French Knots. It was inserted in a purchased frame.

Design by Deborah Lambein.

X	DMC	ANC.	COLOR	X	DMC	¼X	B'ST	ANC.	COLOR
4	209	109	lavender	-	472			253	lt olive
2	210	108	lt lavender	◆	501			878	blue green
⊙	320	215	green	⊙	743			302	yellow
★	334	977	dk blue	+	745	◻		300	lt yellow
△	352	9	peach		801		╱	359	brown
☆	353	6	lt peach	*	962			75	pink
♥	435	1046	tan	⊖	3325	◻		129	blue
■	470	267	dk olive	▢	3716			25	lt pink
V	471	266	olive	•	801		brown French Knot		

Experiencing the miracles that occur every day is part of the wonder of childhood. This simple message of faith makes a nice accent for baby's room.

The design was stitched on a 9" x 10" piece of Antique White Aida (14 ct). Three strands of floss were used for Cross Stitch and 1 strand for Backstitch and French Knots. It was inserted in a purchased frame.

Design by Deborah Lambein.

39w x 49h

X	DMC	ANC.	COLOR
◄	209	109	purple
2	211	342	lt purple
►	353	6	peach
◉	519	1038	blue
✦	744	301	dk yellow
□	745	300	yellow
+	746	275	lt yellow
Π	747	158	lt blue

¼X			

X	DMC	ANC.	COLOR
✱	801	359	brown
◁	912	209	green
◑	955	206	lt green
☆	962	75	dk pink
►	963	73	lt pink
◆	3716	25	pink
●	3772	1007	rose brown

B'ST			
◺	801		brown

¼X			
◹			

French Knot — brown French Knot

95

Building a caring world begins at home. This friendly sign invites friends and neighbors into our lives.

X	DMC	¼X	B'ST	ANC.	COLOR		X	DMC	¼X	B'ST	ANC.	COLOR
•	blanc		✓	2	white		V	680		✓	901	dk gold
♥	310	◢	✓	403	black		☆	806		✓	169	dk blue
✜	321			9046	red		❖	807			168	blue
Σ	666			46	lt red		△	840	◢		379	beige
S	676	◢		891	gold		+	842			388	lt beige
−	677	◢		886	lt gold		✕	3766			167	lt blue

64w x 83h

The design was stitched on a 13" x 14 piece of Ivory Aida (14 ct). Three strands of floss were used for Cross Stitch and 1 strand for Backstitch. It was custom framed.

Design by Kooler Design Studio.

As caretakers of the earth, we are all responsible for nurturing our resources. This angelic design will delight a favorite gardener.

X	DMC	¼X	B'ST	ANC.	COLOR	X	DMC	¼X	B'ST	ANC.	COLOR
•	blanc			2	white	+	801			359	lt brown
Σ	221			897	dk mauve	*	822			390	vy lt beige grey
■	319			218	dk green	⊠	930			1035	dk blue
$	320			215	lt green	✔	931			1034	blue
◉	367			217	green	♡	932			1033	lt blue
V	368			214	vy lt green		938			381	brown
▲	402			1047	lt rust	☆	948			1011	lt flesh
∅	676			891	lt gold	Π	975			355	rust
=	677			886	vy lt gold	★	3032			903	dk beige grey
♥	754			1012	flesh	▽	3033			391	lt beige grey
✦	760			1022	pink	✿	3721			896	mauve
‖	761			1021	lt pink	○	3722			1027	lt mauve
	781			309	dk gold	%	3782			899	beige grey
✕	783			307	gold	⊙	938				brown French Knot

The design was stitched on a 14" square of Natural Aida (14 ct). Three strands of floss were used for Cross Stitch and 1 strand for Backstitch and French Knots. It was custom framed.

Design by Jennifer Lambein.

Prettily bordered with flowers, this "No Smoking" sign issues a polite request for clean air.

The design was stitched on a 9" x 10" piece of Ivory Aida (14 ct). Three strands of floss were used for Cross Stitch and 1 strand for Backstitch and French Knot. It was inserted in a purchased frame (4" x 5" opening).

Design by Kooler Design Studio.

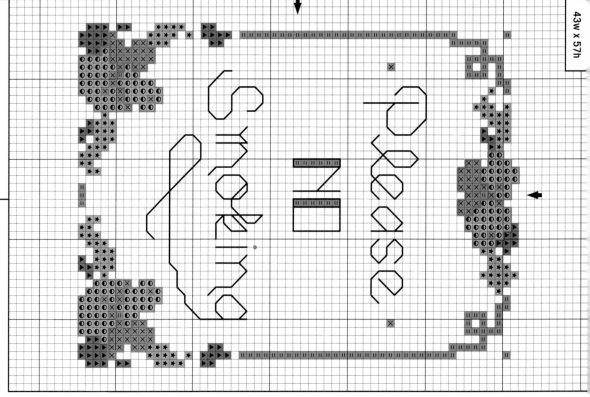

43w x 57h

X	DMC	B'ST	ANC.	COLOR
X	310		403	black
	721		324	lt orange
	900		333	orange
	918		341	dk orange
	3345		268	green
	3347		266	lt green
	310			black French Knot

Accented with a delicate rosebud and a lighthearted message, this coaster is a nice way to thank someone who's gone the extra mile.

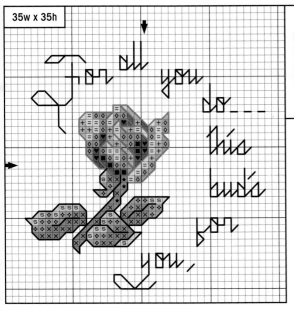

35w x 35h

X	DMC	¼X	B'ST	ANC.	COLOR	X	DMC	¼X	B'ST	ANC.	COLOR
★	319			218	dk green	=	754			1012	lt salmon
❖	320			215	lt green	◇	758			882	salmon
♥	356		✓	5975	vy dk salmon		890		✓	218	vy dk green
✕	367			217	green	+	948			1011	vy lt salmon
S	368			214	vy lt green	■	3778			1013	dk salmon

The design was stitched on an 8" square of Ivory Aida (18 ct).
Two strands of floss were used for Cross Stitch and 1 strand for Backstitch.
It was inserted in a coaster (3½" dia.).

Design by Carol Emmer.

LAUGH
OFTEN

It has been said that laughter is the best medicine for what ails us, and some believe that indulging in a hearty laugh now and again can actually help us live longer, healthier lives. The whimsical pieces in this collection will tickle your soul and bring a smile to your face. An amusing design that features a bewildered bovine, In Greener Pastures *puts a fresh spin on a favorite psalm, giving us a silly reminder that sometimes we just have to take it easy.*

DOWN IN GREEN PASTURES.

PS. 23:2

Design by Rose Calton.

X	1/4X	B'ST	DMC	ANC.	COLOR
	·		blanc	2	white
			225	1026	vy lt pink
	◢		310	403	black
		✳	310	403	black
			318	399	lt grey
			322	978	blue
			334	977	dk blue
			413	401	dk grey
			415	235	grey
			414	398	vy lt grey
			666	46	red
			712	926	cream
			738	361	tan
			739	387	lt tan

X	1/4X	B'ST	DMC	ANC.	COLOR
			744	301	yellow
			760	1022	pink
			761	1021	lt pink
			911	205	dk green
			913	204	green
			3325	129	vy lt blue
			3328	1024	dk pink
			3755	140	lt blue
	◣	✳	3799	236	vy dk grey
			3822	295	dk yellow
✧			blanc		white French Knot
⊞			310		black French Knot

Use long stitches.

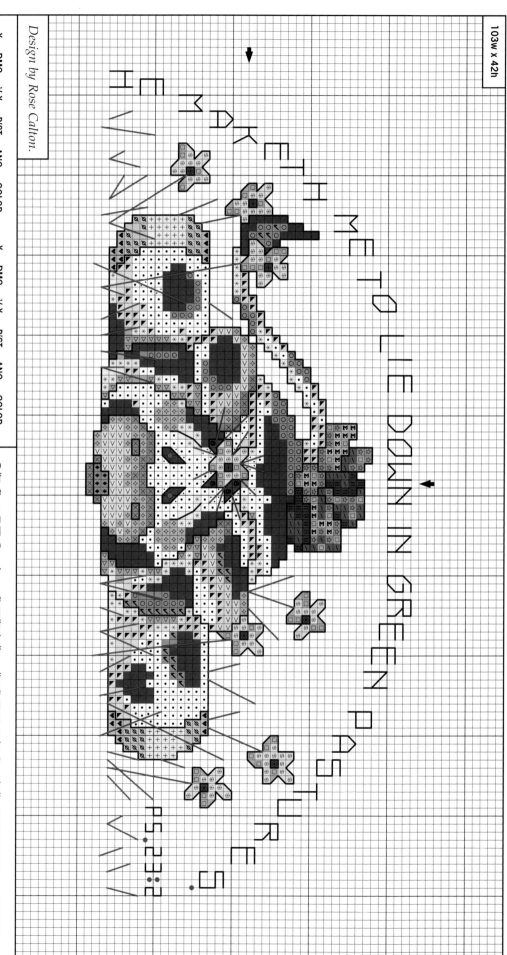

The design was stitched over two fabric threads on a 14" x 10" piece of Antique White Lugana (25 ct). Three strands of floss were used for Cross Stitch, 2 strands for French Knots, Backstitch grass, stems, and wording, and 1 strand for all other Backstitch. It was attached to a purchased pillow.

Note: Use a ¹⁄₂" seam allowance for all seams.

For pillow, trim stitched piece to the desired size and shape plus ¹⁄₂" on all sides for seam allowances. Cut a piece of fabric same size as stitched piece for lining. Baste lining fabric to back of stitched piece close to raw edges.

For cording, cut a 2"w bias strip of fabric the measurement of the outer edge of stitched piece plus 1". Press one end ¹⁄₂" to wrong side. Center ¹⁄₄" dia. cord on the wrong side of bias strip. Matching long edges, fold strip over cord. Using zipper foot, baste along length of strip close to cord; trim seam allowance to ¹⁄₂". Matching raw edges and beginning at center bottom, pin cording to right side of stitched piece. Clip ³⁄₈" into seam allowances at corners. Trim ends of cord to meet. With folded edge on top, overlap fabric over ends of cord. Baste cording in place. Press seam allowances toward wrong side of stitched piece.

To attach stitched piece to pillow, remove stuffing from pillow. Sew stitched piece to pillow front along cording seamline. Restuff pillow and sew opening closed. Embellish as desired.

Delight a youngster with this charming tee. Decked with favorite farmyard friends, it'll let everyone know they're dealing with a real "country kid!"

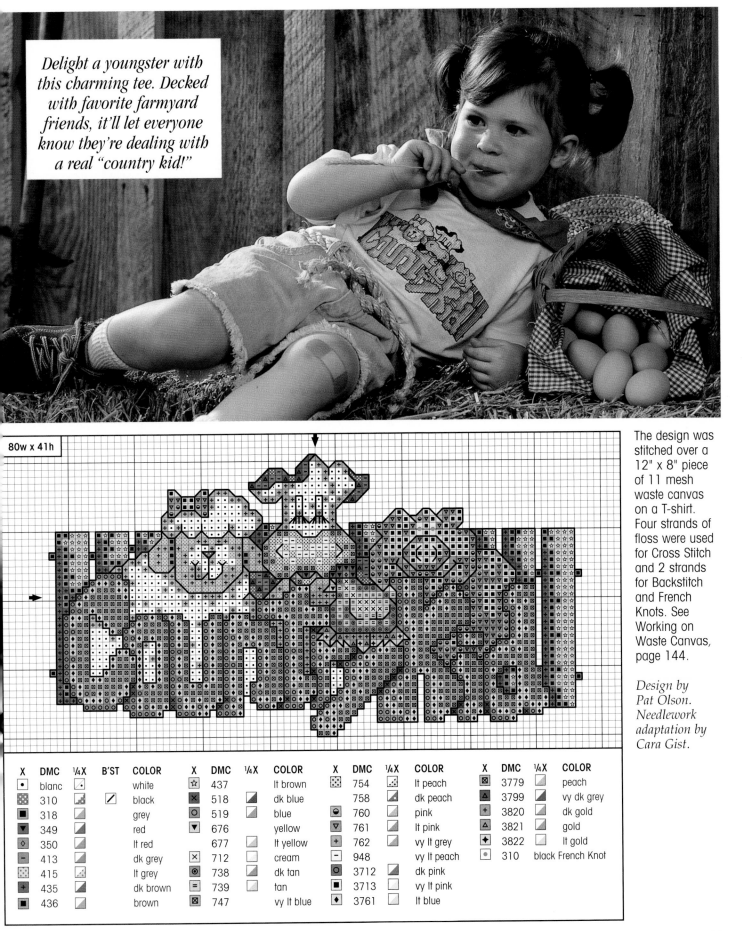

80w x 41h

The design was stitched over a 12" x 8" piece of 11 mesh waste canvas on a T-shirt. Four strands of floss were used for Cross Stitch and 2 strands for Backstitch and French Knots. See Working on Waste Canvas, page 144.

Design by Pat Olson. Needlework adaptation by Cara Gist.

X	DMC	¼X	B'ST	COLOR	X	DMC	¼X	COLOR	X	DMC	¼X	COLOR	X	DMC	¼X	COLOR
•	blanc			white	☆	437		lt brown		754		lt peach	⊠	3779		peach
	310			black	✕	518		dk blue		758		dk peach	▲	3799		vy dk grey
■	318			grey	○	519		blue	⊖	760		pink	+	3820		dk gold
▼	349			red	▼	676		yellow	▽	761		lt pink	△	3821		gold
◇	350			lt red		677		lt yellow	+	762		vy lt grey	✦	3822		lt gold
−	413			dk grey	✕	712		cream	−	948		vy lt peach	⊙	310		black French Knot
	415			lt grey	⊙	738		dk tan	⊙	3712		dk pink				
+	435			dk brown	=	739		tan	■	3713		vy lt pink				
■	436			brown	⊠	747		vy lt blue	✦	3761		lt blue				

105

When life gets to be a zoo, you'll love relaxing in this carefree and comfy sweatshirt. Some of nature's most exotic creatures come to life in the rich colors of this eye-catching design.

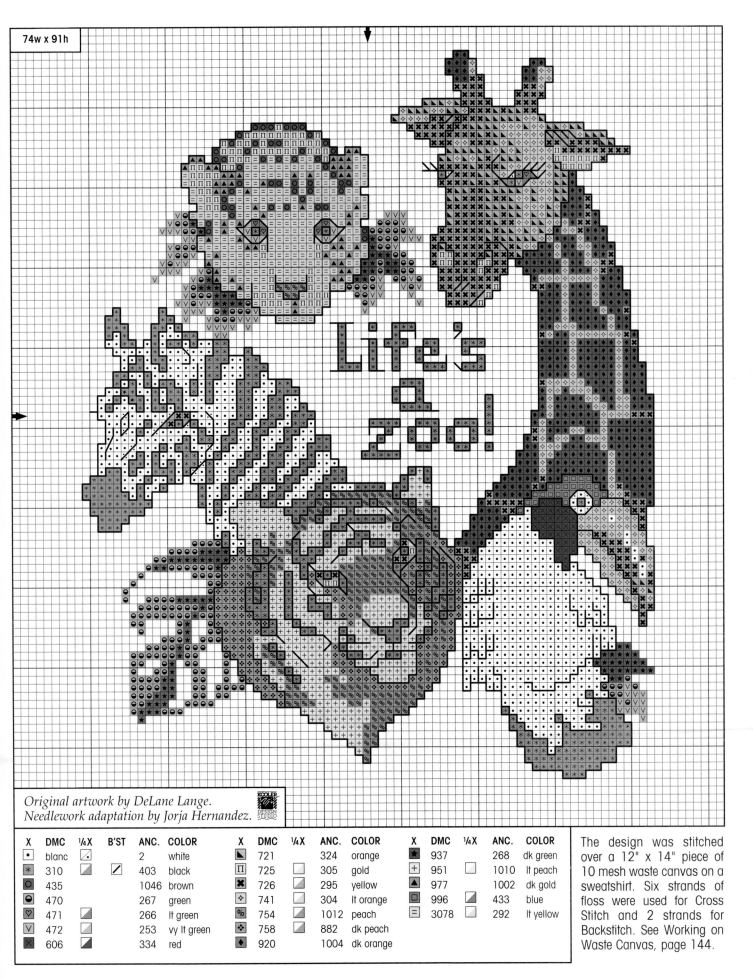

Original artwork by DeLane Lange.
Needlework adaptation by Jorja Hernandez.

KOOLER DESIGN STUDIO

X	DMC	¼X	B'ST	ANC.	COLOR	X	DMC	¼X	ANC.	COLOR	X	DMC	¼X	ANC.	COLOR
•	blanc			2	white		721		324	orange	★	937		268	dk green
*	310		/	403	black	Π	725		305	gold	+	951		1010	lt peach
◎	435			1046	brown	✖	726		295	yellow	▲	977		1002	dk gold
◓	470			267	green	✧	741		304	lt orange	▣	996		433	blue
♡	471			266	lt green	%	754		1012	peach	=	3078		292	lt yellow
V	472			253	vy lt green	✧	758		882	dk peach					
✖	606			334	red	◆	920		1004	dk orange					

The design was stitched over a 12" x 14" piece of 10 mesh waste canvas on a sweatshirt. Six strands of floss were used for Cross Stitch and 2 strands for Backstitch. See Working on Waste Canvas, page 144.

Guests will get a chuckle out of the whimsical warning on this "hoppy" housekeeping sign. Endearing bunnies let it be known that this house is in safe hands!

X	DMC	ANC.	1/4X	B'ST	COLOR
□	762	234			vy lt grey
◁	775	128			lt blue
✳	801	359			brown
◆	3325	129			blue
◀	3328	1024			dk pink
✦	3345	268			dk green
○	3347	266			green
◇	3713	1020			vy lt pink
■	3799	236		◣	charcoal grey

X	DMC	ANC.	1/4X	COLOR
•	blanc	2		white
◀	317	400		vy dk grey
◉	318	399		grey
◑	334	977		dk blue
•	414	235		dk grey
◿	415	398		lt grey
◁	436	1045		tan
☆	437	362		lt tan
★	760	1022		pink
○	761	1021		lt pink

The design was stitched over two fabric threads on a 17" x 14" piece of White Lugana (25 ct). Three strands of floss were used for Cross Stitch and 1 strand for Backstitch. It was custom framed.

Design by DeLane Lange.
Needlework adaptation by Mike Vickery

112w x 71h

This perplexed bear puzzles over the dilemma that any sock-sorter has faced. No matter how many socks go in the wash, there's always one less when they come out!

Sortin' socks isn't hard. It's simple addition.

So how come when the sortin's done, there's always one that's missin'?

74w x 65h

X	DMC	¼X	B'ST	ANC.	COLOR	X	DMC	¼X	B'ST	ANC.	COLOR
⊟	ecru			387	ecru		3031		✓	360	dk brown
▢	223			895	lt pink	d	3032	▢		903	beige
☆	224			893	vy lt pink	2	3033	▨		391	cream
H	501			878	green	▽	3371	◪	✓	382	brown black
✕	503			876	lt green	◆	3721			896	dk pink
✔	676			891	lt gold	◉	3722			1027	pink
✱	729			890	gold		3750		✓	1036	vy dk blue
▲	930	◪		1035	dk blue	★	3781	◪		1050	brown
+	931			1034	blue	♥	3782	◪		899	lt beige
✦	932			1033	lt blue	C	3790	◪		393	dk beige
P	3021	◪		905	dk grey						

The design was stitched over a 13" x 12" piece of 8.5 mesh waste canvas on a muslin laundry bag. Six strands of floss were used for Cross Stitch and 2 strands for Backstitch. See Working on Waste Canvas, page 144.

Design by Carol Emmer.

These quick-as-a-wink magnets will make anyone think sweet thoughts! What a cheery way to say "thank you" or brighten someone's day.

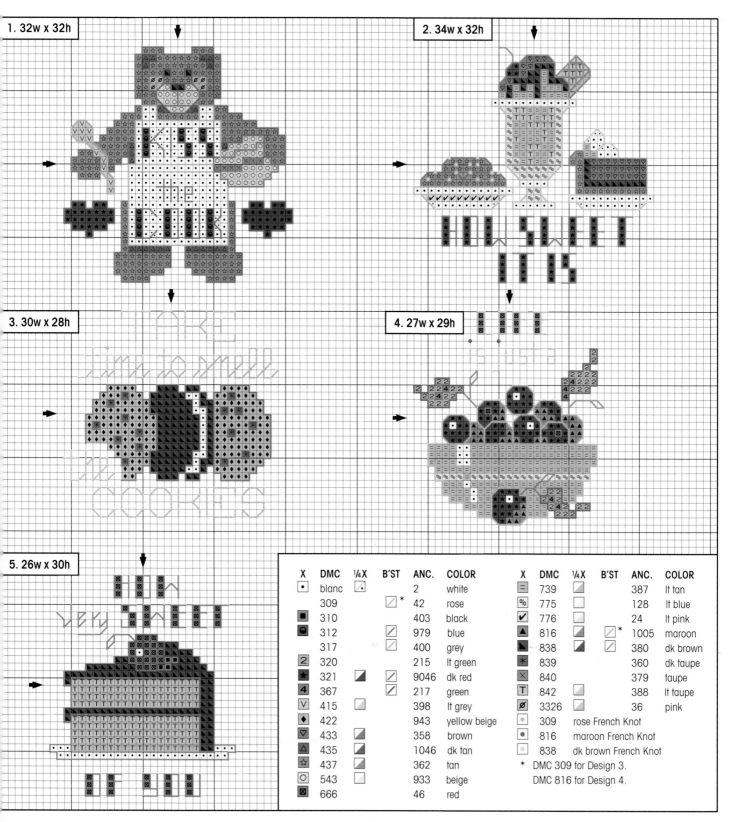

1. 32w x 32h

2. 34w x 32h

3. 30w x 28h

4. 27w x 29h

5. 26w x 30h

X	DMC	1/4X	B'ST	ANC.	COLOR	X	DMC	1/4X	B'ST	ANC.	COLOR
•	blanc			2	white	=	739			387	lt tan
	309		*	42	rose	%	775			128	lt blue
■	310			403	black	✔	776			24	lt pink
◓	312			979	blue	▲	816		*	1005	maroon
	317			400	grey	◣	838			380	dk brown
2	320			215	lt green	✳	839			360	dk taupe
★	321			9046	dk red	✕	840			379	taupe
4	367			217	green	T	842			388	lt taupe
V	415			398	lt grey	∅	3326			36	pink
◆	422			943	yellow beige	•	309				rose French Knot
♡	433			358	brown	•	816				maroon French Knot
△	435			1046	dk tan	•	838				dk brown French Knot
☆	437			362	tan	*	DMC 309 for Design 3.				
O	543			933	beige		DMC 816 for Design 4.				
⊠	666			46	red						

Each design was stitched on a 6" square of Antique White Aida (18 ct). Two strands of floss were used for Cross Stitch and 1 strand for Backstitch and French Knots. They were inserted in round frames (2½" dia. opening). They were made into magnets.

For each magnet, glue magnetic strip to back of frame.

Designs by Kooler Design Studio, Inc.

113

Boost a child's self-esteem by proudly displaying his handiwork. A charming bear artist presents the grand masterpiece with colorful flair.

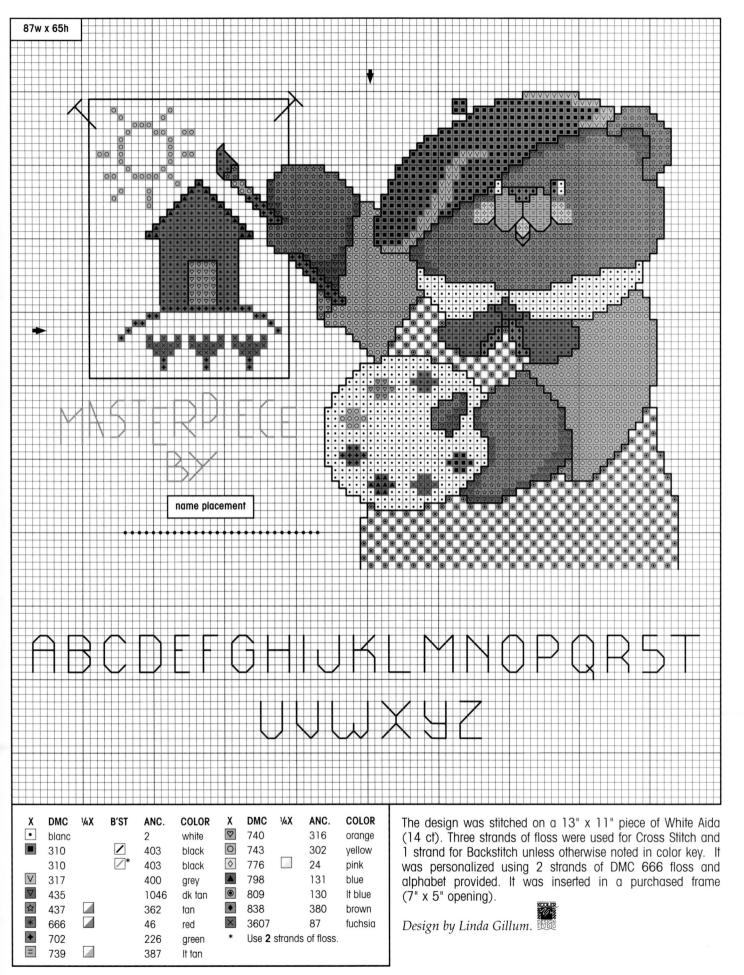

87w x 65h

MASTERPIECE BY

name placement

ABCDEFGHIJKLMNOPQRST
UVWXYZ

X	DMC	¼X	B'ST	ANC.	COLOR	X	DMC	¼X	ANC.	COLOR
•	blanc			2	white	▽	740		316	orange
■	310		╱	403	black	○	743		302	yellow
	310		╱*	403	black	◇	776	☐	24	pink
V	317			400	grey	▲	798		131	blue
▽	435			1046	dk tan	◉	809		130	lt blue
☆	437	◪		362	tan	◆	838		380	brown
✳	666	◪		46	red	✕	3607		87	fuchsia
◆	702			226	green		* Use **2** strands of floss.			
=	739	◪		387	lt tan					

The design was stitched on a 13" x 11" piece of White Aida (14 ct). Three strands of floss were used for Cross Stitch and 1 strand for Backstitch unless otherwise noted in color key. It was personalized using 2 strands of DMC 666 floss and alphabet provided. It was inserted in a purchased frame (7" x 5" opening).

Design by Linda Gillum.

KOOLER DESIGN STUDIO

Good work deserves to be rewarded, and what better way than to show it off! Words of praise, colorfully stitched and finished as magnets, help draw attention to a child's excellent work.

Designs by Linda Gillum.

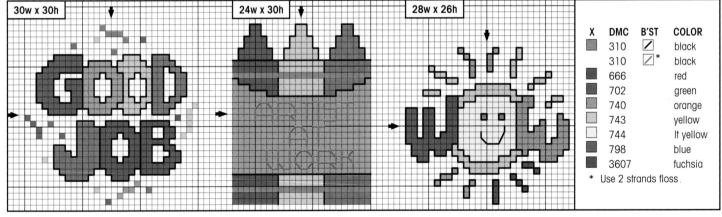

30w x 30h	24w x 30h	28w x 26h

X	DMC	B'ST	COLOR
	310	✓	black
	310	✓*	black
	666		red
	702		green
	740		orange
	743		yellow
	744		lt yellow
	798		blue
	3607		fuchsia

* Use 2 strands floss.

Good Job and **Wow** were each stitched on a 6" square of White Aida (14 ct). Three strands of floss were used for Cross Stitch, and 1 strand for Backstitch. They were inserted in round frames (2½" dia. opening). They were made into magnets.

For each magnet, glue magnetic strip to back of frame.

Artist At Work was stitched on a 6" square of White perforated paper. Three strands of floss were used for Cross Stitch and 1 strand for Backstitch. It was made into a magnet.

For magnet, trim stitched piece as desired. Glue painted clothespin to back of stitched piece. Glue magnetic strip to back of clothespin.

Whether they're happy or sad, clowns always have a way of cheering us up. Why not top a jar of goodies with one of these whimsical fellows and brighten someone's day!

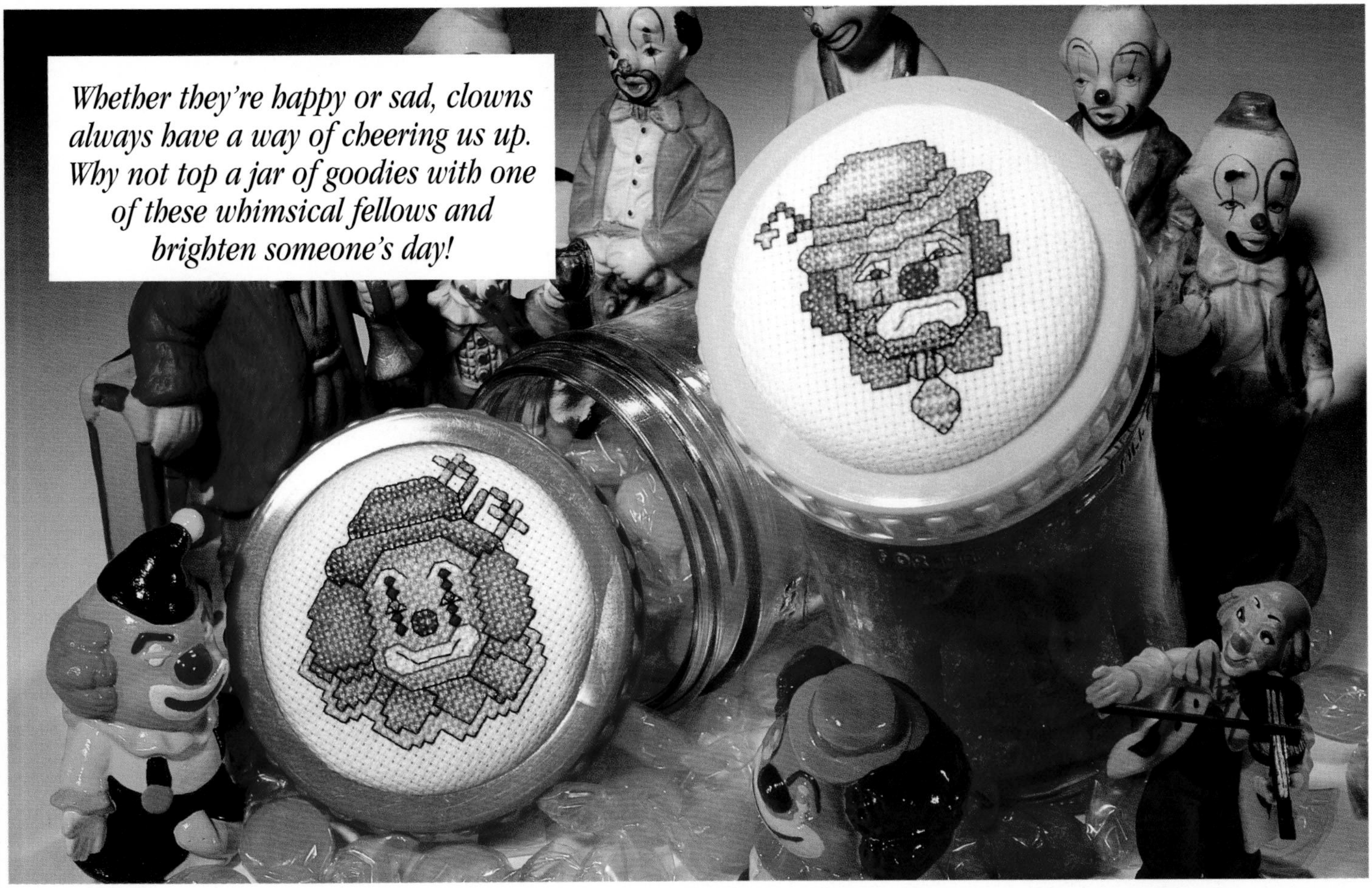

X	DMC	¼X	B'ST	ANC.	COLOR
•	blanc	◪		2	white
■	208	◪		110	dk purple
■	209			109	purple
◒	210			108	lt purple
■	304	◪		1006	dk red
◆	321		⧄	9046	red
4	402	◪		1047	peach
★	433	◪		358	dk brown
5	434	◪		310	brown
B	436	◪		1045	lt brown
△	597	◪		168	blue
◆	598			167	lt blue
N	645	◪		273	grey
☆	647	◪		1040	lt grey
◉	677			886	lt gold
+	680	◪		901	dk gold
C	701	◪		227	green
V	703			238	lt green
×	721			324	orange
2	722			323	lt orange
Π	729	◪		890	gold
-	743	◪		302	dk yellow
*	744			301	yellow
❖	920	◪		1004	rust
3	922			1003	lt rust
S	945	◪		881	lt peach
	3371		⧄	382	brown black
•	blanc	white French Knot			

28w x 33h

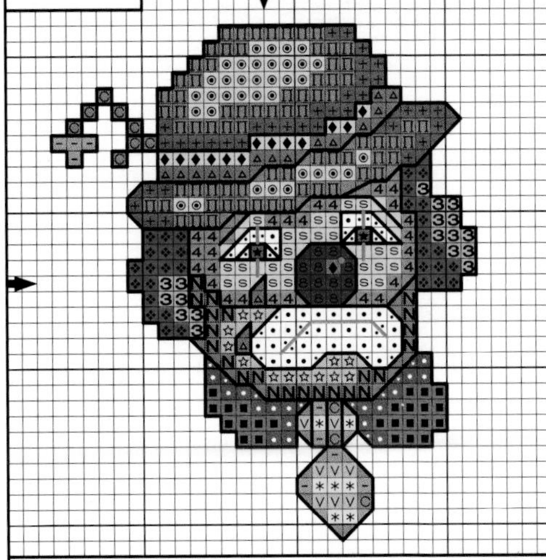

28w x 34h

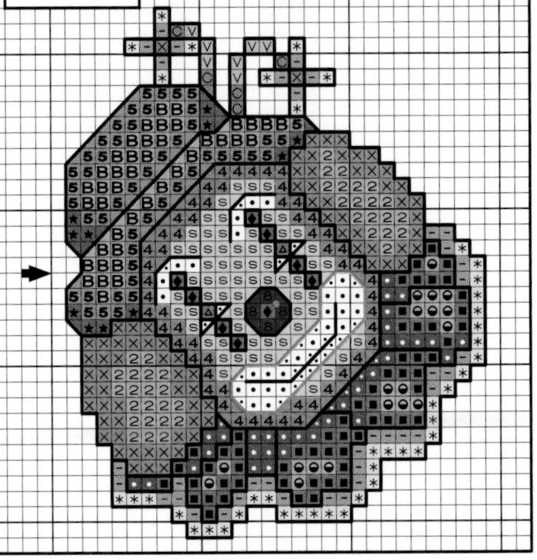

Each design was stitched on a 7" square of White Aida (14 ct). Two strands of floss were used for Cross Stitch and 1 strand for Backstitch and French Knots. They were inserted in wide-mouth jar lids.

For jar lid, use **outer edge** of jar lid for pattern and draw a circle on adhesive mounting board. Cutting slightly inside drawn line, cut out circle. Using **opening** of jar lid for pattern, cut a circle of batting. Center batting on adhesive side of board and press in place. Center stitched piece on batting and press edges onto adhesive board; trim edges close to board. Glue board inside jar lid. (**Note:** Mason jar puff-up kits may be used to finish jar lids.)

Designs by Lorraine Birmingham.

When things start to go haywire, a bit of humor often helps put matters back into perspective! This design will bring a chuckle whenever life gets a little crazy.

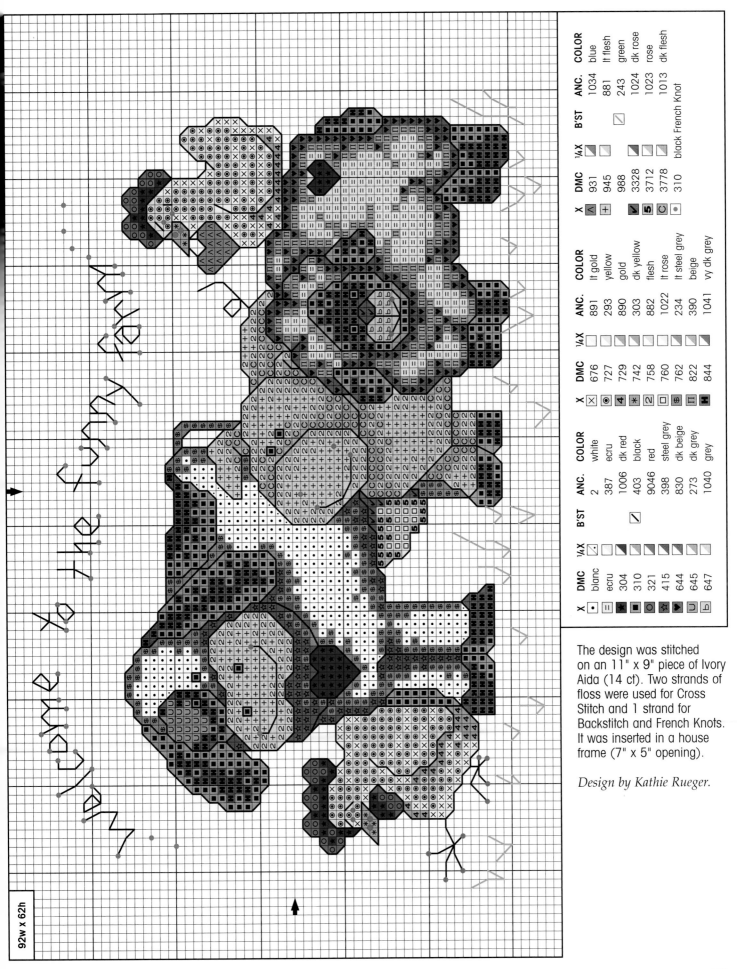

X	DMC	ANC.	COLOR
<	931	1034	blue
+	945	881	lt flesh
	988	243	green
	3328	1024	dk rose
5	3712	1023	rose
C	3778	1013	dk flesh
•	310		black French Knot

X	DMC	ANC.	COLOR
X	676	891	lt gold
⊙	727	293	yellow
4	729	890	gold
*	742	303	dk yellow
2	758	882	flesh
□	760	1022	lt rose
$	762	234	lt steel grey
Π	822	390	beige
H	844	1041	vy dk grey

X	DMC	ANC.	COLOR
•	blanc	2	white
=	ecru	387	ecru
★	304	1006	dk red
■	310	403	black
O	321	9046	red
☆	415	398	steel grey
▶	644	830	dk beige
U	645	273	dk grey
Ь	647	1040	grey

92w x 62h

The design was stitched on an 11" x 9" piece of Ivory Aida (14 ct). Two strands of floss were used for Cross Stitch and 1 strand for Backstitch and French Knots. It was inserted in a house frame (7" x 5" opening).

Design by Kathie Rueger.

Sometimes pet-lovers let their priorities get a bit topsy-turvy. These playful designs let us know that furry friends come first in this house!

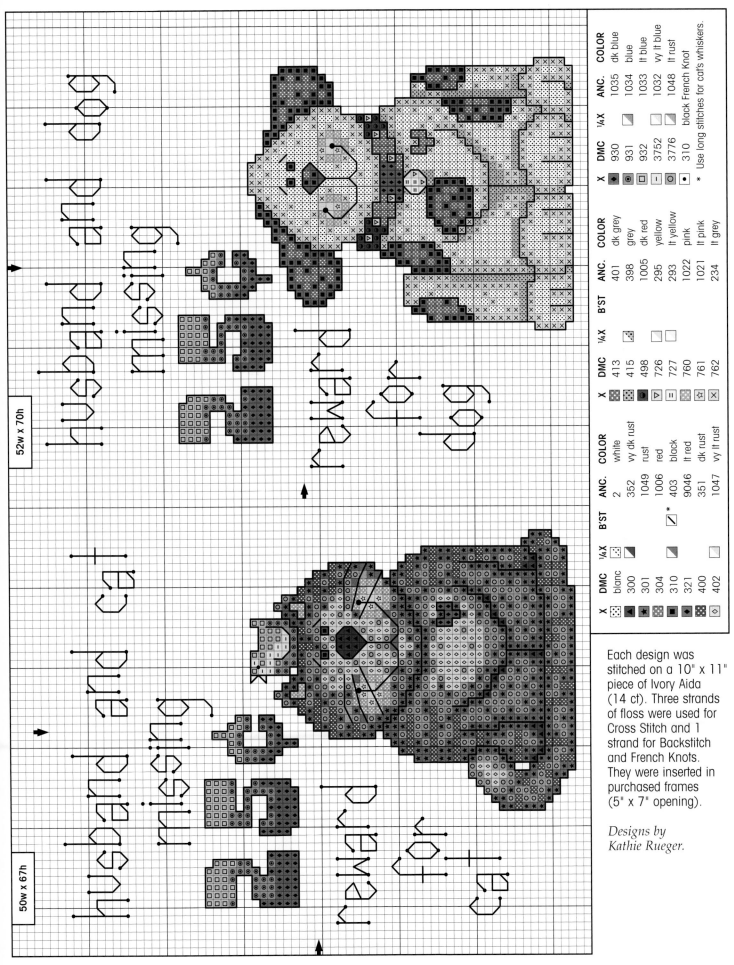

X	DMC	ANC.	COLOR
	930	1035	dk blue
	931	1034	blue
	932	1033	lt blue
	3752	1032	vy lt blue
	3776	1048	lt rust
	310		black French Knot

* Use long stitches for cat's whiskers.

X	DMC	ANC.	COLOR
	413	401	dk grey
	415	398	grey
	498	1005	dk red
	726	295	yellow
	727	293	lt yellow
	760	1022	pink
	761	1021	lt pink
	762	234	lt grey

X	DMC	ANC.	COLOR
	blanc	2	white
	300	352	vy dk rust
	301	1049	rust
	304	1006	red
	310	403	black
	321	9046	lt red
	400	351	dk rust
	402	1047	vy lt rust

52w x 70h

50w x 67h

Each design was stitched on a 10" x 11" piece of Ivory Aida (14 ct). Three strands of floss were used for Cross Stitch and 1 strand for Backstitch and French Knots. They were inserted in purchased frames (5" x 7" opening).

Designs by Kathie Rueger.

Rain, rain, go away — and don't come back another day! Noah's delightful friends send us a wishful message from the front of this snuggly sweatshirt.

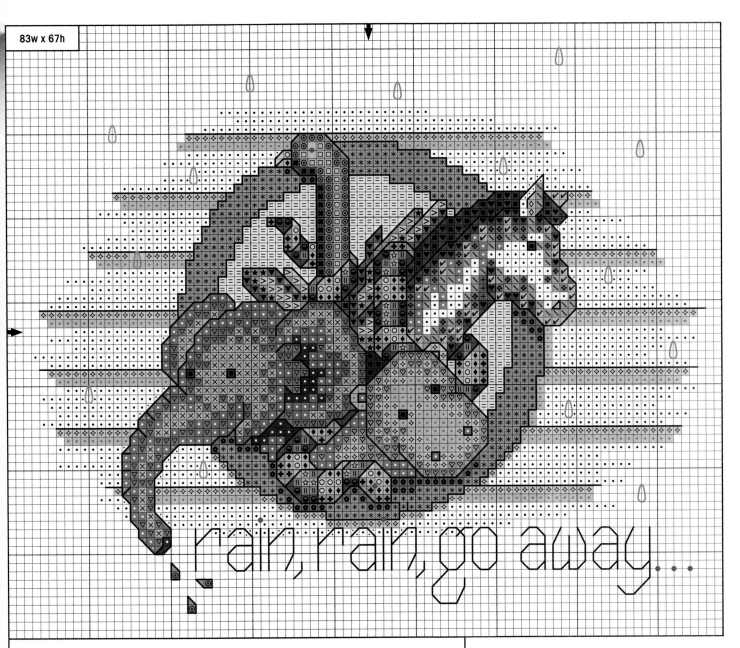

X	DMC	¼X	B'ST	ANC.	COLOR	X	DMC	¼X	ANC.	COLOR
•	blanc			2	white	◎	743		302	yellow
◣	ecru			387	ecru	=	744		301	lt yellow
▼	208			110	dk lavender	◇	761		1021	lt pink
★	209			109	lavender	✕	762		234	lt grey
>	210			108	lt lavender	✳	798		131	dk blue
■	310		✓	403	black	□	799		136	lt blue
⊡	318			399	steel grey	◉	809		130	blue
⬠	347			1025	red	✚	842		388	beige
◼	414			235	dk grey	♥	844		1041	vy dk beige grey
▽	415			398	grey	◖	910		229	dk green
✔	543			933	lt beige	‖	911		205	green
❖	645			273	dk beige grey	☆	913		204	lt green
⊟	646			8581	beige grey	·	3072		847	pearl grey
♡	647			1040	lt beige grey	✱	3328		1024	pink
◈	648			900	vy lt beige grey	•	310			black French Knot
✚	741			304	orange	⊘	799			lt blue Lazy Daisy
◆	742			303	lt orange					

The design was stitched over a 14" x 12" piece of 8.5 mesh waste canvas on a T-shirt. Six strands of floss were used for Cross Stitch and 2 strands for Backstitch, French Knots, and Lazy Daisy stitches. See Working on Waste Canvas, page 144.

Design by Jane Chandler.

A tender teddy and a chubby bunny are playful reminders that babies need lots of hugs! The simple design is easy to stitch on a soft onesie for a last-minute shower gift.

X	DMC	¼X	B'ST	COLOR	X	DMC	¼X	B'ST	COLOR
•	blanc			white		801			brown
	335		/	dk rose		899			rose
	413		/	grey		954			green
★	435			tan		955			lt green
	437			lt tan		3608			fuchsia
△	776			lt rose		3609			lt fuchsia
♡	800			lt blue					

The design was stitched over a 7" square of 14 mesh waste canvas on a onesie. Three strands of floss were used for Cross Stitch and 1 strand for Backstitch. See Working on Waste Canvas, page 144.

Design by Linda Gillum.

40w x 43h

Grandmother will love wearing this fun T-shirt! Its lighthearted message jokingly "cautions" others that she's ready at any time to share proud stories and pictures of her grandchildren.

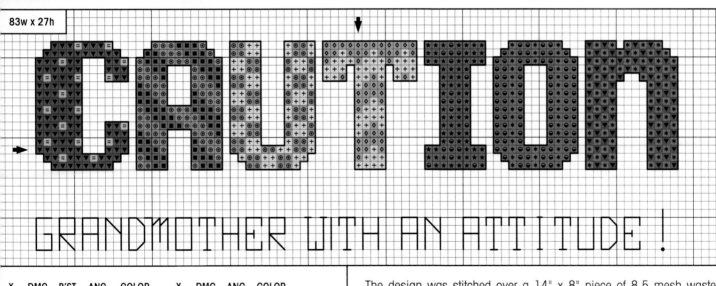

83w x 27h

X	DMC	B'ST	ANC.	COLOR	X	DMC	ANC.	COLOR
	310	✓*	403	black	◉	740	316	orange
✳	553		98	purple	+	743	302	yellow
▼	666		46	red	◙	798	131	blue
★	701		227	green	=	961	76	pink
◇	703		238	lt green	•	310		black French Knot
■	718		88	fuchsia	*	Use 4 strands for backstitch words.		

The design was stitched over a 14" x 8" piece of 8.5 mesh waste canvas on a T-shirt. Six strands of floss were used for Cross Stitch, 2 strands for Backstitch unless otherwise noted in color key, and 4 strands for French Knot. See Working on Waste Canvas, page 144.

Design by Polly Carbonari.

Posted in an entryway, this whimsical sign is sure to elicit lots of smiles — it warns visitors to not only watch out for the dog, but to beware of the children, too!

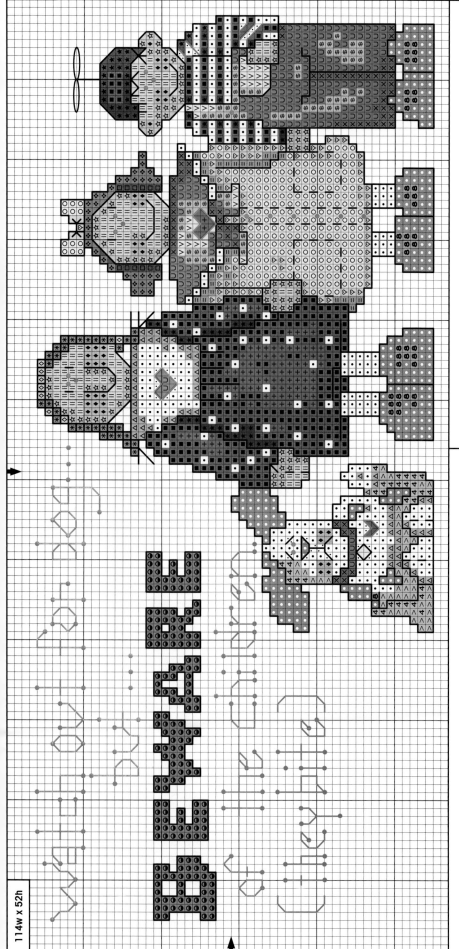

X	1/4X	B'ST	DMC	ANC.	COLOR
			815	43	vy dk red
			822	390	lt beige
			844	1041	dk grey
			930	1035	dk blue
			931	1034	blue
			932	1033	lt blue
		*	3750	1036	vy dk blue
			3752	1032	vy lt blue
			3779	868	peach
			304		dk red French Knot
			310		black French Knot
			3750		vy dk blue French Knot
			310		black Lazy Daisy
*					Use 2 strands of floss for French Knots and Backstitch words.

X	1/4X	B'ST	DMC	ANC.	COLOR
			blanc	2	white
			304	1006	dk red
			310	403	black
			321	9046	red
			434	310	brown
			435	1046	lt brown
			610	889	dk tan
			611	898	tan
			644	830	beige
			666	46	lt red
			743	302	dk yellow
			744	301	yellow
			745	300	lt yellow
			754	1012	lt peach
			760	1022	rose
			762	234	grey

114w x 52h

The design was stitched on a 14" x 10" piece of Ivory Aida (14 ct). Three strands of floss were used for Cross Stitch and 1 strand for Backstitch, French Knots, and Lazy Daisy stitches unless otherwise noted in color key. It was inserted in a purchased frame (10" x 5" opening).

For frame, use a foam brush to apply blue acrylic paint; immediately wipe off paint with a clean soft cloth. Allow paint to dry. Trace heart pattern onto tracing paper and cut out. Referring to photo for placement, draw around heart pattern across top and bottom of frame. Paint hearts using a small brush and red acrylic paint; allow paint to dry. Use a black fine-point permanent marker to draw a dashed line around outside edge of each heart. Spray frame with matte clear acrylic sealer.

Design by Kathie Rueger.
Needlework adaptation by Kathy Werkmeister.

Organize your snapshots and mementos inside this "toad-aly" awesome covered album. Our darling duo adds a lovable touch to a photo album or scrapbook.

69w x 74h

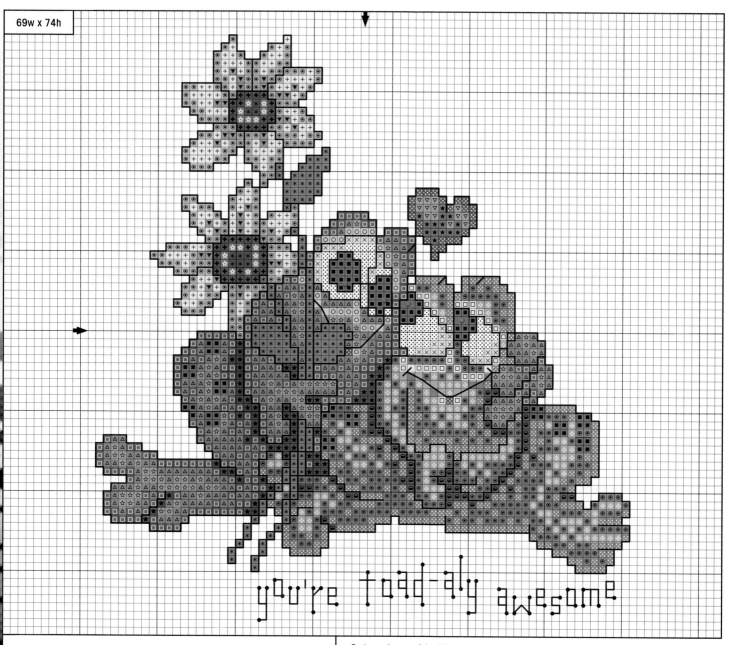

X	DMC	B'ST	COLOR	X	DMC	COLOR
▨	blanc		white	✳	700	dk yellow green
■	310	/	black	◉	725	dk yellow
◨	319		vy dk grey green	+	727	lt yellow
◉	320		grey green	✕	762	lt grey
★	321		lt red	▼	783	gold
▨	367		dk grey green	★	986	dk green
◇	368		lt grey green	◱	987	green
◻	369		vy lt grey green	△	988	lt green
✦	433		vy dk brown	☆	3347	olive green
☆	434		dk brown	○	3348	lt olive green
✳	435		brown	•	blanc	white French Knot
▨	498		red	●	310	black French Knot
▽	666		vy lt red			

The design was stitched on an 11" x 12" piece of Antique White Aida (14 ct). Three strands of floss were used for Cross Stitch, 2 strands for French Knots, and 1 strand for Backstitch. It was made into a photo album.

For album cover, cut a 26" x 14½" piece of fabric to cover a 10¼"w x 11¾"h purchased album with a 2½" spine.

Cut a piece of batting same size as opened album. Glue batting to album. Press edges of fabric ½" to wrong side. Place fabric wrong side up on flat surface. Open album and center on fabric. Beginning at one short edge of fabric, glue ½" of fabric to inside of album. Fold and glue long edges to inside of album. Glue remaining short edge of fabric to inside of album. Cut two pieces of thick paper smaller than inside of album; glue to inside of album, covering edges of fabric.

For stitched piece, cut mounting board desired shape. Using board as a guide, cut a paper pattern ¾" larger than board on all sides. Centering pattern on design, cut out stitched piece. Clip ¼" into edges of stitched piece at ½" intervals. Cut batting same size as board; place on board. Place stitched piece on batting; fold and glue edges to back of board.

For cording, cut a 2"w bias strip of fabric the measurement of the outer edge of board plus 1". Center ¼" dia. cord on the wrong side of bias strip. Fold strip over cord. Using zipper foot, baste along length of strip close to cord; trim seam allowance to ½". Pin cording to back of board along outer edge. Opening ends of cording, cut cord to fit exactly. Insert one end of cording in the other; turn top end under ½". Glue cording to back of board along outer edge. Glue board to front of album.

Design by Kathie Rueger.

Everyone loves the fruits of the garden — even our produce-picking penguin! This eager eater dons her bonny bonnet and gets ready for the harvest.

90w x 96h

X	DMC	½X	B'ST	ANC.	COLOR	X	DMC	ANC.	COLOR	X	DMC	½X	ANC.	COLOR
•	blanc			2	white	•	415	398	pearl grey		761		1021	lt salmon
◣	ecru			387	ecru	▼	434	310	dk brown	✕	762		234	lt pearl grey
◨	304			1006	dk red	★	435	1046	brown	▢	775		128	lt blue
◼	310		╱	403	black	‖	437	362	lt brown		3325	◉	129	lt baby blue
▽	318			399	grey	⬠	725	305	dk yellow	▪	3799		236	dk grey
◆	321			9046	red	○	726	295	topaz	✳	3820		306	gold
✖	322			978	blue	+	727	293	yellow	•	3823		386	lt yellow
=	334			977	baby blue	▣	738	361	tan	⊘	321			red Lazy Daisy
✦	367	♥		217	green	♡	739	387	cream					
✔	368	▦		214	lt green	―	760	1022	salmon					

The design was stitched over two fabric threads on a 15" x 16" piece of Antique White Lugana (25 ct). Three strands of floss were used for Cross Stitch and 1 strand for Backstitch, Half Cross Stitch, and Lazy Daisy stitches. It was custom framed.

Design by Ursula Wollenberg.

These three little piggies know that a well-fed family is a happy family! The plump trio will be pleased to find a place in a country kitchen or breakfast nook.

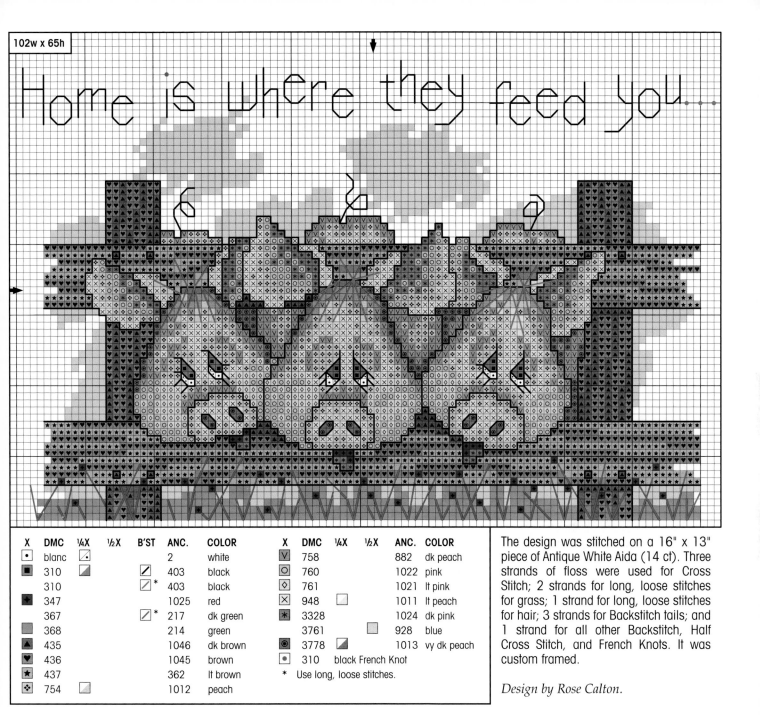

X	DMC	¼X	½X	B'ST	ANC.	COLOR
•	blanc	⊡			2	white
■	310	◨		◪	403	black
	310			◪ *	403	black
★	347				1025	red
	367			◪ *	217	dk green
	368				214	green
▲	435				1046	dk brown
♥	436				1045	brown
★	437				362	lt brown
❖	754	◩			1012	peach

X	DMC	¼X	½X	ANC.	COLOR
V	758			882	dk peach
O	760			1022	pink
◇	761			1021	lt pink
✕	948	▢		1011	lt peach
✱	3328			1024	dk pink
	3761		▢	928	blue
◉	3778		◪	1013	vy dk peach
•	310			black French Knot
*	Use long, loose stitches.

The design was stitched on a 16" x 13" piece of Antique White Aida (14 ct). Three strands of floss were used for Cross Stitch; 2 strands for long, loose stitches for grass; 1 strand for long, loose stitches for hair; 3 strands for Backstitch tails; and 1 strand for all other Backstitch, Half Cross Stitch, and French Knots. It was custom framed.

Design by Rose Calton.

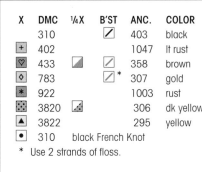

Fashioned with a simple moon and star motif, our celestial framed piece will make an "out-of-this-world" gift.

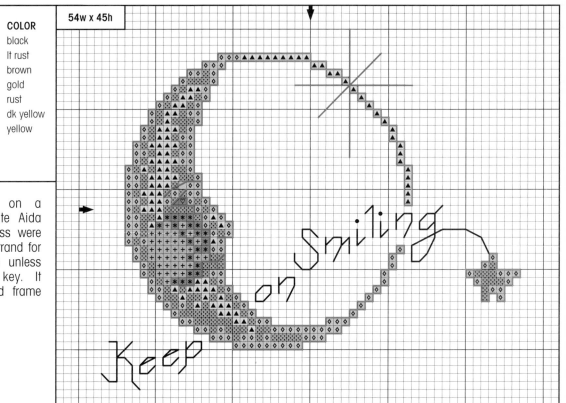

X	DMC	¼X	B'ST	ANC.	COLOR
	310		╱	403	black
+	402			1047	lt rust
♡	433	◪	╱	358	brown
◇	783	◪	╱ *	307	gold
✳	922			1003	rust
▦	3820	◪		306	dk yellow
▲	3822			295	yellow
●	310				black French Knot

* Use 2 strands of floss.

54w x 45h

The design was stitched on a 10" square of Antique White Aida (14 ct). Three strands of floss were used for Cross Stitch and 1 strand for Backstitch and French Knots unless otherwise noted in color key. It was inserted in a purchased frame (5" x 4" opening).

Design by Sandi Gore Evans. Needlework adaptation by Jane Chandler.

Summertime brings out the fanciful child in all of us. So go ahead, forget your worries and enjoy life — just for the fun of it!

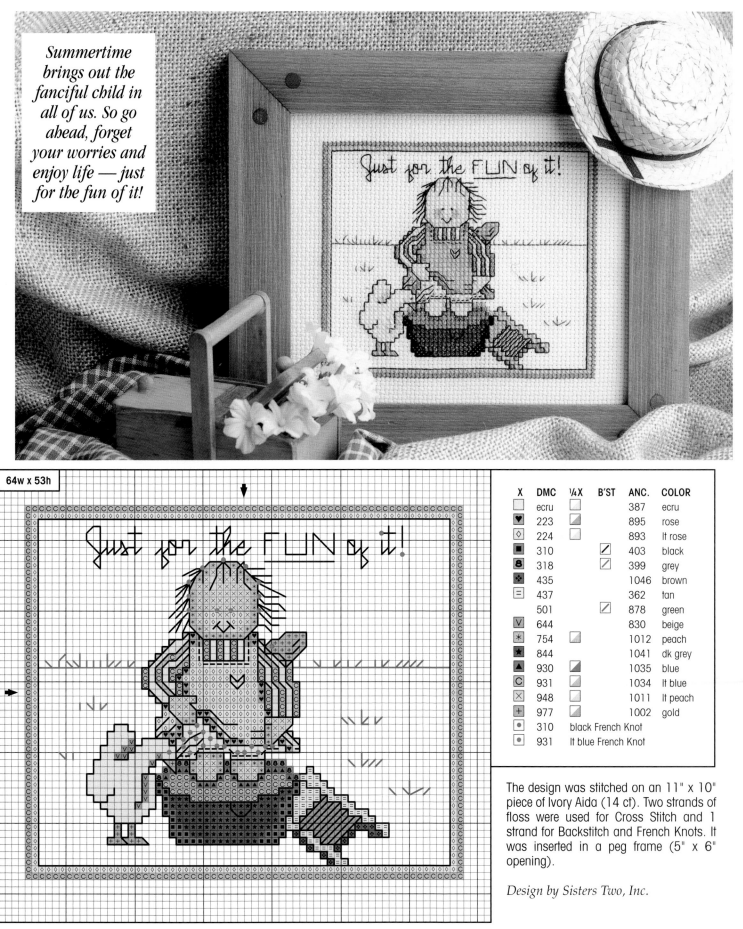

64w x 53h

X	DMC	¼X	B'ST	ANC.	COLOR
	ecru			387	ecru
♥	223			895	rose
◊	224			893	lt rose
■	310		╱	403	black
8	318		╱	399	grey
✿	435			1046	brown
=	437			362	tan
	501		╱	878	green
V	644			830	beige
*	754			1012	peach
★	844			1041	dk grey
▲	930			1035	blue
C	931			1034	lt blue
×	948			1011	lt peach
+	977			1002	gold
•	310				black French Knot
•	931				lt blue French Knot

The design was stitched on an 11" x 10" piece of Ivory Aida (14 ct). Two strands of floss were used for Cross Stitch and 1 strand for Backstitch and French Knots. It was inserted in a peg frame (5" x 6" opening).

Design by Sisters Two, Inc.

ring bell for maid service....

if no answer do it yourself....

Busy moms will especially appreciate our household humor. After all, when help's not around — or too tired to answer — folks might just have to help themselves!

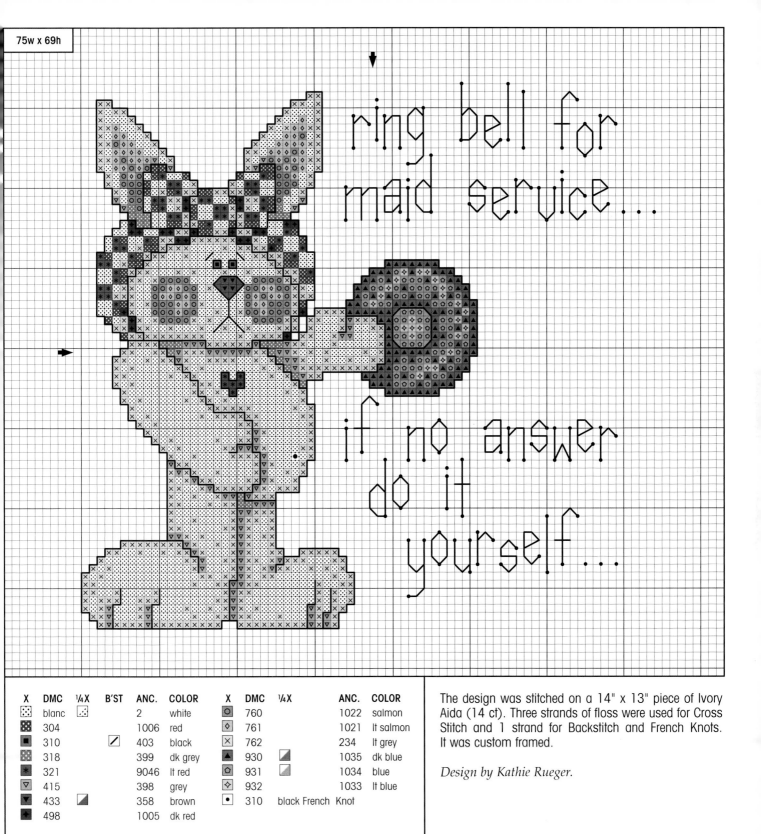

75w x 69h

ring bell for maid service...

if no answer do it yourself...

X	DMC	¼X	B'ST	ANC.	COLOR		X	DMC	¼X		ANC.	COLOR
	blanc			2	white			760			1022	salmon
	304			1006	red			761			1021	lt salmon
	310			403	black			762			234	lt grey
	318			399	dk grey			930			1035	dk blue
	321			9046	lt red			931			1034	blue
	415			398	grey			932			1033	lt blue
	433			358	brown			310			black French Knot	
	498			1005	dk red							

The design was stitched on a 14" x 13" piece of Ivory Aida (14 ct). Three strands of floss were used for Cross Stitch and 1 strand for Backstitch and French Knots. It was custom framed.

Design by Kathie Rueger.

This comical tee will make a great treat for a friend who needs a little encouragement. Quick to stitch, the long-legged frog and his inspiring words remind us that success isn't always easy!

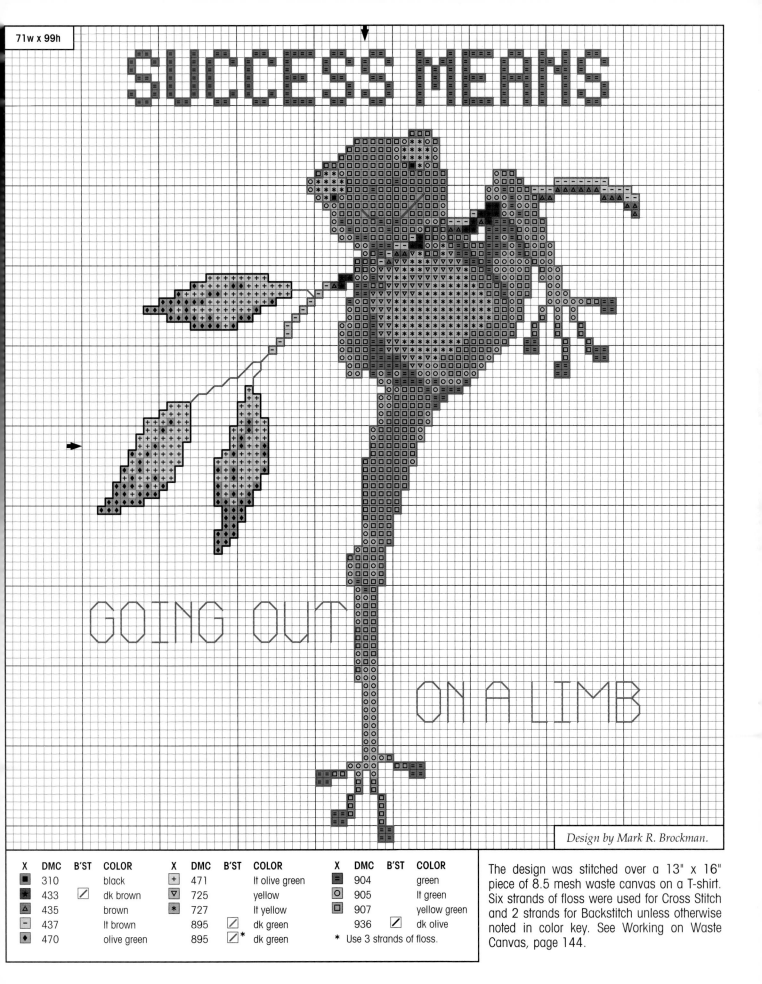

SUCCESS MEANS

GOING OUT

ON A LIMB

Design by Mark R. Brockman.

X	DMC	B'ST	COLOR	X	DMC	B'ST	COLOR	X	DMC	B'ST	COLOR
■	310		black	+	471		lt olive green	▬	904		green
★	433	✓	dk brown	▽	725		yellow	○	905		lt green
△	435		brown	*	727		lt yellow	□	907		yellow green
-	437		lt brown		895	✓	dk green		936	✓	dk olive
◆	470		olive green		895	✓*	dk green			*	Use 3 strands of floss.

The design was stitched over a 13" x 16" piece of 8.5 mesh waste canvas on a T-shirt. Six strands of floss were used for Cross Stitch and 2 strands for Backstitch unless otherwise noted in color key. See Working on Waste Canvas, page 144.

139

"Purr-fect" for a cat lover, this design proudly proclaims an affection for felines. The tender sentiment is highlighted by the kitty's captivating eyes.

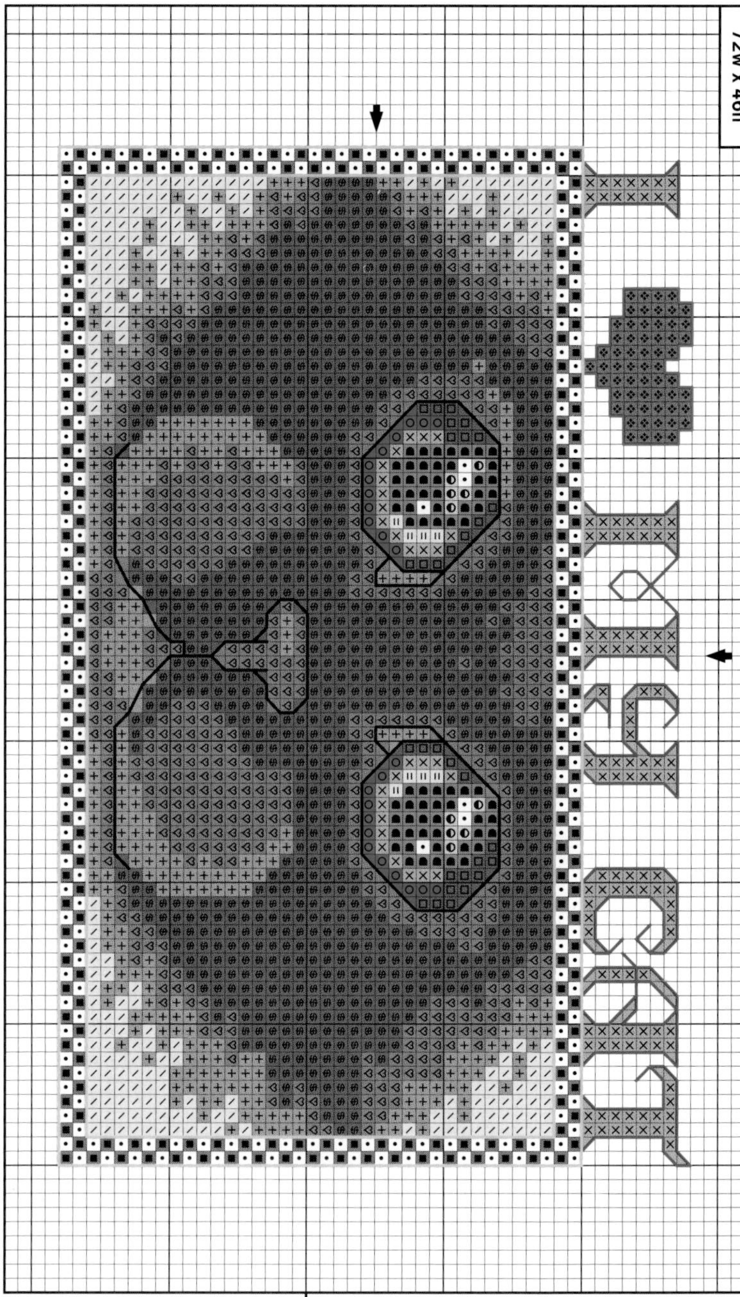

The design was stitched over a 13" x 10" piece of 8.5 mesh waste canvas on a T-shirt. Six strands of floss were used for Cross Stitch and 2 strands for Backstitch. See Working on Waste Canvas, page 144.

X	DMC	¼X	B'ST	COLOR
•	blanc			white
/	ecru			ecru
◖	310	◪	◪	black
◘	312	◪	◪	dk blue
◐	318			grey
❖	326		◪	pink
X	519	◪		lt blue
=	828			vy lt blue
$	839	◪		dk brown
◁	840	◪		brown
+	841	◪		lt brown
O	3760	◪		blue
■	3799		◪	dk grey

Design by Barbara Baatz.

Want to boost your beau's ego or let a handsome acquaintance know you have your eye on him? Surprise him with this "good look'n" mug!

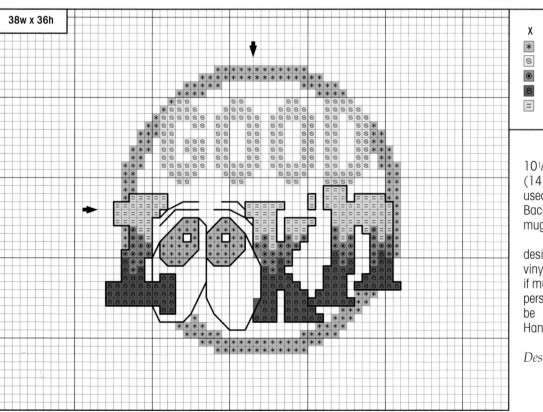

38w x 36h

X	DMC	¼X	B'ST	ANC.	COLOR
✳	310	◪	◿	403	black
S	435			1046	tan
◉	813			161	blue
8	826			161	dk blue
=	828			9159	lt blue

The design was stitched on a 10¼" x 3½" piece of Vinyl-Weave™ (14 ct). Two strands of floss were used for Cross Stitch and 1 strand for Backstitch. It was inserted in a white mug.

For design placement, center design 3" from one short edge of vinyl. Stitch design at right end of vinyl if mug is to be used by a right-handed person or on the left end if mug is to be used by a left-handed person. Hand wash mug to protect stitchery.

Design by Sam Hawkins.

141

Design by Kooler Design Studio.

The design was stitched over two fabric threads on a 16" x 14" piece of Antique White Lugana (25 ct). Three strands of floss were used for Cross Stitch and 1 strand for Backstitch. It was custom framed.

X	DMC	¼X	B'ST	ANC.	COLOR	X	DMC	¼X	B'ST	ANC.	COLOR	X	DMC	¼X	B'ST	ANC.	COLOR
•	blanc	◹		2	white	☆	722	◹		323	orange	T	988	◹	◹*	243	green
	309		◹*	42	dk rose	\	738	◹		361	tan	✧	3024	◹		397	grey
	310	◹	◹*	403	black	O	743	◹		302	yellow	$	3760	◹		169	blue
▽	335	◹	◹*	38	rose	⊠	744	◹		301	lt yellow	U	3766	◹		167	lt blue
■	350	◹		11	dk peach	*	772			259	lt green	◉	3776	◹		1048	rust
≡	352			9	peach	+	776			24	pink	* DMC 309 for lettering. DMC 310 for eyes.					
✕	353			6	lt peach	C	801		◹*	359	brown	DMC 335 for hearts. DMC 517 for birds					
◇	402	◹		1047	lt rust	‖	818			23	lt pink	and blue flowers.					
	413		◹†	401	dk grey	>	828			9159	vy lt blue	† DMC 413 for pink flowers and birds.					
	517		◹*	162	dk blue	▼	899			52	dk pink	DMC 561 for lettering.					
✦	561	◹	◹†	212	blue green	◼	975	◹	◹	355	dk rust	* DMC 801 for nest and branch.					
4	704	◹		256	bright green	✪	986	◹	◹	246	dk green	DMC 988 for tendrils.					

GENERAL INSTRUCTIONS

WORKING WITH CHARTS

How to Read Charts: Each of the designs is shown in chart form. Each colored square on the chart represents one Cross Stitch or one Half Cross Stitch. Each colored triangle on the chart represents one One-Quarter Stitch or one Three-Quarter Stitch. Black or colored dots represent French Knots. Black or colored ovals represent Lazy Daisy Stitches. The straight lines on the chart indicate Backstitch. When a French Knot, Lazy Daisy Stitch, or Backstitch covers a square, the symbol is either omitted or a reduced symbol is shown.

Each chart is accompanied by a color key. This key indicates the color of floss to use for each stitch on the chart. The headings on the color key are for Cross Stitch (**X**), DMC color number (**DMC**), One-Quarter Stitch (**¼X**), Three-Quarter Stitch (**¾X**), Half Cross Stitch (**½X**), Backstitch (**B'ST**), Anchor color number (**ANC**), and color name (**COLOR**). Color key columns should be read vertically and horizontally to determine type of stitch and floss color.

How to Determine Finished Size: The finished size of your design will depend on the thread count per inch of the fabric being used. To determine the finished size of the design on different fabrics, divide the number of squares (stitches) in the width of the charted design by the thread count of the fabric. For example, a charted design with a width of 80 squares worked on 14 count Aida will yield a design 5¾" wide. Repeat for the number of squares (stitches) in the height of the charted design. (**Note:** To work over two fabric threads, divide the number of squares by one-half the thread count.) Then add the amount of background you want, plus a generous amount for finishing.

Where to Start: The horizontal and vertical centers of the charted design are shown by arrows. You may start at any point on the charted design, but be sure the design will be centered on the fabric. Locate the center of fabric by folding in half, top to bottom and again left to right. On the charted design, count the number of squares from the center of the chart to the determined starting point; then, from the fabric's center, count out the same number of fabric threads.

STITCH DIAGRAMS

Counted Cross Stitch (X): For horizontal rows, work stitches in two journeys (**Fig. 1**). For vertical rows, complete each stitch as shown (**Fig. 2**). When working over two fabric threads, work Cross Stitch as shown in **Fig. 3**. When the chart shows a Backstitch crossing a colored square (**Fig. 4**), a Cross Stitch should be worked first; then the Backstitch (**Fig. 9 or 10**) should be worked on top of the Cross Stitch.

Fig. 1

Fig. 2

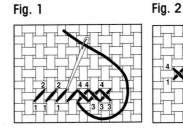

Fig. 3

Fig. 4

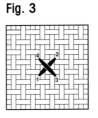
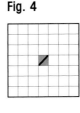

Quarter Stitch (¼X and ¾X): Come up at 1 (**Fig. 5**); then split fabric thread to go down at 2. When stitches 1-4 are worked in the same color, the resulting stitch is called a Three-Quarter Stitch (**¾X**). When working over 2 fabric threads, work Quarter Stitches as shown in **Fig. 6**.

Fig. 5

Fig. 6

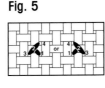
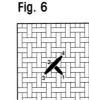

Half Cross Stitch (½X): This stitch is one journey of the Cross Stitch and is worked from lower left to upper right as shown in **Fig. 7**. When working over two fabric threads, work Half Cross Stitch as shown in **Fig. 8**.

Fig. 7

Fig. 8

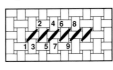

Backstitch (B'ST): For outline detail, Backstitch should be worked after the design has been completed (**Fig. 9**). When working over two fabric threads, work Backstitch as shown in **Fig. 10**.

Fig. 9

Fig. 10

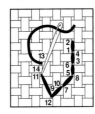
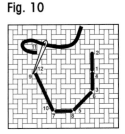

French Knot: Bring needle up at 1. Wrap floss once around needle and insert needle at 2, holding floss with non-stitching fingers (**Fig. 11**). Tighten knot; then pull needle through fabric, holding floss until it must be released. For larger knot, use more strands; wrap only once.

Fig. 11

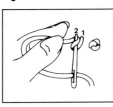

Lazy Daisy Stitch: Bring needle up at 1 and make a loop. Go down at 1 and come up at 2, keeping floss below point of needle (**Fig. 12**). Pull needle through and go down at 2 to anchor loop, completing stitch. (**Note:** To support stitches, it may be helpful to go down in edge of next fabric thread when anchoring loop.)

Fig. 12

STITCHING TIPS

Working over Two Fabric Threads: Use the sewing method instead of the stab method when working over two fabric threads. To use the sewing method, keep your stitching hand on the right side of the fabric (instead of stabbing the fabric with the needle and taking your stitching hand to the back of the fabric to pick up the needle). With the sewing method, you take the needle down and up with one stroke instead of two. To add support to stitches, it is important that the first Cross Stitch is placed on the fabric with stitch 1-2 beginning and ending where a vertical fabric thread crosses over a horizontal fabric thread (**Fig. 13**). When the first stitch is in the correct position, the entire design will be placed properly, with vertical fabric threads supporting each stitch.

Fig. 13

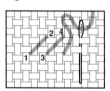

Working on Waste Canvas: Waste canvas (also known as tear-away cloth or waste cloth) is a special canvas that provides an evenweave grid for placing stitches on fabric. After the design is worked over the canvas, the canvas threads are removed, leaving the design on the fabric. Most canvas has blue parallel threads every fifth square to aid in counting and in placing the canvas straight on the fabric. The blue threads may be placed horizontally or vertically. The canvas is available in several mesh sizes. Use lightweight, nonfusible interfacing on wrong side of fabric to provide a firmer stitching base. We recommend a screw-type hoop that is large enough to encircle the entire design. Use a #24 tapestry needle for knit fabric. Use a sharp embroidery needle for tightly knit or tightly woven fabric. To ensure smoother stitches, separate floss strands and realign them before threading the needle.

Step 1. Cut waste canvas 2" larger than design size on all sides. Cut interfacing same size as canvas. To prevent raw edges of canvas from marring fabric, cover edges of canvas with masking tape.

Step 2. Find desired placement for design; mark center of design on garment with a pin.

Step 3. Match center of canvas to pin. Use the blue threads in canvas to place canvas

straight on garment; pin canvas to garment. Pin interfacing to wrong side of garment. To prevent canvas from slipping, especially on large designs, baste securely around edge of canvas through all three thicknesses. Then baste from corner to corner and from side to side as shown in **Fig. 14**.

Fig. 14

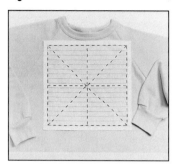

Step 4. Place garment in hoop. The hoop helps keep the area not being stitched out of the way. Roll excess fabric, including back of garment, over top edge of hoop and pin in place (**Fig. 15**).

Fig. 15

Step 5. Work design following chart and Stitch Diagrams.

Step 6. Trim canvas to within ³/₄" of design. Use a sponge or spray bottle of water to dampen canvas until it becomes limp. Using tweezers, pull out canvas threads one at a time (**Fig. 16**).

Fig. 16

Step 7. Trim interfacing close to design.

FINISHING TECHNIQUES
FOOTPRINTS

Continued from page 17.
Footprints should be applied to fabric before design is stitched. To make footprint template, cut a 15" square of tracing paper. Measure 4" from center bottom of tracing paper; mark with a pencil. Matching marking on tracing paper to center bottom of charted design, place tracing paper over chart; trace footprints. Cut out footprints along traced lines. Matching edges, pin template to fabric. Pour approximately 1 teaspoon acrylic paint onto paper plate; add 1 to 2 drops of water to paint and stir with toothpick. Dab sponge brush into thinned paint; use brush to lightly paint bottom of baby's foot. Gently press foot onto fabric within cut out area of template. Repeat for other footprint.

PILLOW FINISHING

Continued from page 35.
Note: Use a ¹/₂" seam allowance for all seams.

For pillow front, trim stitched piece to 7" x 6". Cut backing fabric same size as stitched piece.

For fabric and lace ruffle, match right sides and short edges of a 5" x 53" piece of fabric. Sew short edges together; press seam open. With wrong sides together, match raw edges and press ruffle in half. Sew short edges of a 53" length of 2"w flat lace together; press seam open. Matching raw edges of ruffle and straight edge of lace, baste ³/₈" and ¹/₄" from raw edge. Pull basting threads, gathering ruffle to fit edge of pillow front. Matching raw edges, pin ruffle to right side of pillow front over cording; baste in place.

Matching right sides and leaving an opening for turning, sew stitched piece and backing fabric together. Trim corners diagonally; turn pillow right side out. Stuff pillow with fiberfill; sew final closure by hand.